The Twelve Birds of Christmas

THE TWELVE BIRDS
OF CHRISTMAS

Stephen Moss

◼ SQUARE PEG

3 5 7 9 10 8 6 4 2

Square Peg, an imprint of Vintage,
20 Vauxhall Bridge Road,
London SW1V 2SA

Square Peg is part of the Penguin Random House group of companies whose
addresses can be found at global.penguinrandomhouse.com

Penguin
Random House
UK

First published by Square Peg in 2019

Penguin.co.uk/vintage

A CIP catalogue record for this book is available from the British Library

ISBN 9781529110104

Typeset by Dinah Drazin

Printed and bound by Clays Ltd, Elcograf S.p.A.

Penguin Random House is committed to a sustainable future for our
business, our readers and our planet. This book is made from
Forest Stewardship Council® certified paper.

MIX
Paper from
responsible sources
FSC® C018179

*To two dear friends: my agent, Broo Doherty, and my editor,
Graham Coster, with grateful thanks for their advice, support
and friendship over the years.*

On the twelfth day of Christmas,
my true love sent to me
Twelve drummers drumming,
Eleven pipers piping,
Ten lords a-leaping,
Nine ladies dancing,
Eight maids a-milking,
Seven swans a-swimming,
Six geese a-laying,
Five gold rings,
Four colly birds,
Three French hens,
Two turtle doves,
And a partridge in a pear tree!

Contents

Introduction

'The Twelve Days of Christmas' is, in many ways, the best-known of all our Christmas carols. It may not have the gravitas of 'Once in Royal David's City', the poignancy of 'In the Bleak Midwinter', or the sheer, rousing energy of 'O Come, All Ye Faithful', but it is probably heard – and sung – more often than any of them. Endlessly parodied, highly memorable and occasionally infuriating, it perfectly captures the spirit of the festive season.

There have been dozens of recorded versions, from Burl Ives to Connie Francis, and the Vienna Boys' Choir to John Denver and the Muppets. Even Frank Sinatra had a go, although he decided to replace the familiar lines with his own versions, including 'three golf clubs, two silken scarfs and a most lovely lavender tie'.

But like other well-known 'counting songs', such as 'Ten Green Bottles' and 'One Man Went to Mow', this is not a composition to listen to. Rather, it should be sung, loudly and heartily, usually accompanied by the familiar melody composed by Frederic Austin in 1909. Once you hear that famous opening line – 'On the first day of Christmas, my true love gave to me' – it takes quite an effort to resist singing the next: 'A partridge in a pear tree . . .'

In this book, *The Twelve Birds of Christmas*, I look beneath the surface of this familiar carol, and reveal what I believe is an alternative meaning to the verses. For in my view, every single one of the carol's dozen lines could plausibly be about a particular species of bird.

'The Twelve Days of Christmas' first appeared in written form around the year 1780. I have a facsimile copy of the very first example, which comes from a selection of popular verses for children entitled *Mirth without Mischief*. The book's printing is crude and messy, and the lettering old-fashioned and unfamiliar, with the letter 's' represented as 'f', as was the custom of the day. Yet it is still possible to make out the verses, now so familiar, but then, presumably, truly fresh and original. The only difference is that in this early version the order of the verses is slightly different from the modern one, with 'Twelve lords-a-leaping' and 'Eleven ladies dancing', instead of 'Twelve drummers drumming' and 'Eleven pipers piping'.

The song first appeared in print during this period, but, like any poem or song in the oral tradition, its origins surely go back much further in time.

The concept of 'the twelve days of Christmas' is one of the earliest of all Christian ideas, and may have its roots even earlier, with the pagan midwinter festival of Yule, associated with the Norse god Odin. The early Christian church adopted the idea with enthusiasm, with the period known as Christmastide running from 25 December – Christmas Day itself – to 5 January.

The days and nights were dominated by celebration, feasting

and merrymaking, culminating in 'Twelfth Night' (commemorated in Shakespeare's play of the same name). The aim was to ward off the gloom and darkness of winter and herald the new year to come, with the tantalisingly distant promise of spring.

'The Twelve Days of Christmas', with its jollity and easy-to-remember verse pattern, must have fitted the festive mood rather well. It has been suggested that the gifts it speaks of may even have been intended to be presented at a wedding between the two lovers, with the partridge and the pear tree symbolising sex and love.

But could the verses actually have a much darker side? Some commentators have claimed that it may have been written during the sixteenth-century Reformation, the period of religious upheaval that pitched traditional Catholics against arriviste Protestants, tearing Europe apart. Far from being a light-hearted diversion, they suggest, the song has a deadly serious purpose: to teach young Catholic children the Catechism, a summary of their deep religious faith. The theory is that it was written, in code, by a desperate group of English Catholics who were being ruthlessly oppressed by the new Protestant queen, Elizabeth. Their plight was extreme: they ran the constant risk of imprisonment, torture, or even the unimaginable agony of being burned at the stake.

If we look at the carol's verses as a series of hidden symbols, then, could the 'three French hens' actually represent the Trinity, the 'four colly birds' the Gospels, the 'lords-a-leaping' the Ten Commandments, and the 'drummers drumming' the twelve disciples?

It is of course quite possible that there is a hidden religious

3

meaning in the words. But, given that the first four lines, together with the sixth and seventh, explicitly refer to birds, might the real meaning behind the song actually turn out to be not sacred, but avian?

I have no definitive proof for my case. That's because, as with so many folk songs and carols, we have no written evidence of the origins of 'The Twelve Days of Christmas' – only the words themselves. I do, however, believe my own – admittedly rather whimsical – interpretation is at least as plausible as any other.

After all, having conclusively proved that the first seven verses refer to birds, it seems unlikely to me that none of the remaining five would. In any case, how exactly would you go about giving someone ten real-life lords or eight milkmaids?

Birds certainly dominate the first few verses: not just that oddly arboreal partridge, but also 'two turtle doves' and 'three French hens'. 'Four colly birds' is a bit of a mystery, and what about 'five gold rings'? It is natural to assume that this refers to jewellery, but it has been claimed that the line is about blackbirds (which have a gold ring around their eye), or even pheasants (a white ring around their neck). As we shall discover, though, I believe the verse refers to a very different bird.

'Six geese a-laying' and 'seven swans a-swimming' appear to be the only other avian gifts – but are they? Could, indeed, every gift – and verse – actually feature a bird?

Birds could also be represented in at least two other verses (drummers drumming and pipers piping – woodpeckers and sandpipers respectively); while for the remaining three (lords

a-leaping, ladies dancing and maids a-milking), I have come up with what I believe to be plausible explanations for an ornithological origin.

The alternative – that the gifts in lines eight to twelve (milkmaids, ladies, lords, pipers and drummers) are, quite literally, groups of human beings, seems to me to be very unlikely indeed.

Roast turkey aside, it's perhaps not surprising that birds should feature in a celebration of Christmas. After all, any gift of large, edible species such as swans or geese, or even smaller ones like turtle doves and partridges, would surely in those days have been intended for the oven, as part of the Christmas feast?

This utilitarian attitude certainly prevailed at the time the carol was written. But there is a more spiritual side to this relationship, too. Birds have long been regarded as the most visible and familiar aspect of the natural world. Many species have over time acquired symbolic qualities, such as the linking of doves with love and fidelity; a connection that stretches from the earliest cultures all the way down to the present day. So, what could be more natural than for a man (or woman, for this is a rare example of a narrator who could be of either sex) to sing of twelve bird-based gifts, presented by his or her 'true love'? This does not necessarily mean that each bird would be trussed up and handed over: what is important is the symbolic meaning behind each gift.

However we choose to interpret the meaning of each verse, one thing is certain: delivering all the gifts would cost a pretty penny. In 1984, an enterprising member of staff at PNC Bank, based in the US city of Pittsburgh, calculated that if all the presents mentioned in the song were bought (or hired) on the open market, the suitor would need to pay out $12,623.10 – then roughly £8,400.

Since then, the bank has recalculated the sum required each year: the most recent figure, for 2018, comes to $39,094.93 – about £30,000. Some economists believe that this so-called 'Christmas Price Index' is actually a better reflection of rises in the cost of living than the official ones!

Coincidentally, the late eighteenth century – when the carol first appeared in print, and so became available to a much wider audience than before – was a significant period in our understanding and appreciation of British birds and other wildlife. This was largely thanks to the publication, in 1789, of a modest little volume: *The Natural History of Selborne*.

Written by a Hampshire vicar, the Revd Gilbert White, *Selborne* (as it is usually known) was not only the first book of its kind, documenting the natural history of a single, familiar location, but also by far the most popular, and has been constantly in print in the two centuries or so since it first appeared.

White was an acute observer, whose notes and diaries have proved incredibly valuable to later generations of naturalists, as they often indicate how common – or rare – a particular species was more than two centuries ago. That's a crucial date, as it represents the start of the agricultural and industrial revolutions that have so transformed our land and its wildlife. I shall be quoting from White, and many of his later followers, throughout this book, as I trace the fortunes of the birds featured in the verses of the carol since it first appeared in the late eighteenth century.

I have long been fascinated by the social, historical and cultural aspects of our relationship with birds – a field I have already explored in my biographies *The Robin* and *The Wren*. Now, in *The Twelve Birds of Christmas*, I set out to map this relationship more widely. I shall be weaving history, culture, folklore and the science of bird behaviour into a narrative about twelve of our best-known, and best-loved, species of bird. Along the way, I shall be examining how the fortunes of each of these dozen birds have ebbed and flowed over time.

Ultimately, I hope that this book offers a light-hearted way of interpreting a rather puzzling carol, and helps the reader discover new aspects about the biological and cultural lives of birds.

Stephen Moss
Mark, Somerset
April 2019

A Partridge in a Pear Tree

GREY PARTRIDGES

The rival nineteenth-century ornithologists George Montagu, William MacGillivray and William Yarrell did not always see eye-to-eye. But on one thing they could firmly agree: that the native, common, grey or 'English' partridge would be so familiar to their readers that it was hardly worth describing in any detail.

'This species is so well known as to require very little description . . .'; 'It might be judged unnecessary to describe a bird so common as the Partridge . . .'; 'Of a bird so universally known, little that is new can be said . . .' The openings of the three naturalists' accounts are so similar it almost feels as if they were copying one another, like lazy children plagiarising a classmate's homework.

Such casual dismissal of this once-familiar rural bird highlights a major deficiency in our attitudes to wildlife, and especially to common species. We tend to take them more or less for granted, often ignoring them in favour of more glamorous, and rarer, birds such as the avocet or osprey. It's true that we only began to notice species like the house sparrow, starling, cuckoo and skylark when it finally dawned on us that they had started to vanish from their traditional haunts. Of few birds is this truer than the grey partridge.

Less than half a century ago, the first comprehensive nation-wide survey of our breeding birds, the British Trust for Ornithology's 1968–72 *Atlas*, estimated that there might be as many as half a million pairs of partridges in Britain and Ireland. In his 2005 work *Birds Britannica*, Mark Cocker reported that this had fallen to 75,000 pairs.

Since then, things have got even worse. The latest estimate suggests that there are now just 43,000 pairs remaining – a decline of over 90 per cent in less than half a century, earning the species an unwanted place near the very top of the Red List of Birds of Conservation Concern. At this rate, scientists predict that by the middle of the current century – perhaps even earlier – the grey partridge could disappear entirely from our countryside.

Nowadays it is almost impossible for us to imagine just how common and familiar this quintessential bird of the British countryside used to be, as recently as the time of our parents' or grandparents' childhood. In his wartime book *Watching Birds*, James Fisher made a brave stab at listing Britain's commonest species. Taking songbirds out of the equation (smaller birds have, on average, bigger populations than larger ones), he ranked the grey partridge as second only to the wood pigeon as our com-monest bird, with roughly the same numbers as the mallard or the moorhen.

When I was growing up in the late 1960s and early 1970s, I remember seeing large groups of partridges in the fields around south-east England, crouched still and low like clods of earth as they tried to avoid being seen. During a visit to the huge concrete bowl of a new reservoir being built on the western edge of London, on a hot summer's day in 1974, I inadvertently flushed a family of partridges. I recall how the adults raced away ahead of me, frantically followed by their still flightless chicks.

Even as late as the 1980s and 1990s, when I went birding in the Home Counties I would regularly come across partridges, while no trip to Norfolk or Suffolk was complete without seeing large flocks scattered across fields of sugar beet or potatoes. But by the turn of the millennium, I could spend a whole week in East Anglia without coming across a single one. If I did find partridges at all, they would invariably be the gaudy red-legged variety – more about this alien incomer later.

A clue to the reason why the grey partridge, this once-ubiquitous bird of our lowland countryside, has suffered such a precipitous decline comes, ironically, from a period when it was still one of the commonest of all rural birds. In the second volume of the long-running Collins New Naturalist series, *British Game*, published in 1946, the countryman Brian Vesey-Fitzgerald recalled an old country proverb: 'Good farming and partridges go hand in hand.' That was certainly true from the early nineteenth century, when agriculture switched away from traditional strip-farming to a patchwork of enclosed, hedge-bound fields, until the eve of the Second World War.

Ironically, as William Yarrell pointed out in 1843, the rise in the grey partridge's fortunes only happened because of the increased number and dominance of human beings, and the associated developments in farming technology:

The enlarged demands of an increasing population, the tempting prices of seasons of scarcity, or the progress of science unfolding the nature of spoils, have each in turn induced the cultivation of various tracts of ground unploughed before; and as the labours of the agriculturist encroach on the boundaries of the moor, the Grouse retires, and the Partridge takes its place upon the land.

In other words, just what the old proverb said: good farming and partridges go hand-in hand. Note, however, that little word *good*. And now consider the effect that 'bad' farming has had: not just on the grey partridge, but on a whole suite of Britain's rural birds, including the skylark, yellowhammer, linnet, corn bunting and, the subject of the next chapter, the (by now surely doomed) turtle dove.

Later in this chapter I shall examine just why modern intensive agriculture, and the headlong pursuit of higher yields of arable crops, is so incompatible with the partridge's way of life. But first, for those readers unfamiliar with the bird, a brief description of its appearance and habits.

Like so many birds which, from a distance, appear grey or brown, a partridge, when you have a good view of it, is revealed as a creature of subtle but exquisite grace. It may not have the bright hues of a kingfisher; it may be rather plump and squat; but the partridge is still a bird of great beauty. The body is indeed grey, but on close examination it can be seen that this is actually made up of dark, wavy 'vermiculations' (from the Latin word for worm) running across a lighter background.

On the partridge's back and wings, that grey background is almost obliterated by broad, chestnut-brown streaks, which look as if they have been casually daubed by a wayward child. The bird's face and throat, meanwhile, are of a lighter, almost orange hue. Most strikingly, when the male turns towards the observer, he reveals a large, dark-brown, horseshoe-shaped mark, delicately fringed with white, on his lower breast. And when a grey partridge takes to the wing, it reveals russet-coloured sides to the tail. As William MacGillivray rightly noted: 'Though neither elegant in form, nor gaudily attired, its neatness, and the curiously intricate markings of its plumage, entitle it to be considered a beautiful bird.'

Female grey partridges are slightly drabber than males, in order to stay camouflaged when incubating their eggs, but still show the same basic colours and pattern. Yet, even though he was so familiar with the species, Brian Vesey-Fitzgerald confessed that despite having 'lived in good partridge country all my life . . . I should not care to say that I could always say which was which.' He did note, however, that the male partridge often adopts a more alert, upright posture than his mate when on the move, perhaps because he is on the constant lookout for danger.

Both male and female partridges are pot-bellied in shape, looking rather like a plump skittle, and weigh about 400 grams (about 14 ounces). They have short legs, a small, down-curved bill and a longish neck, which helps them see above the surrounding vegetation, so they can watch for any approaching danger.

That's essential, for few birds are quite as vulnerable as the partridge. These birds spend the vast majority of the time on the

ground, making them very susceptible to opportunistic predators like foxes, badgers, stoats and rats, and aerial ones such as raptors, which prey on the nesting females. Crows and rooks are also a perennial danger, as they are able to take eggs and young chicks.

The poet John Clare beautifully evoked the latent fear that must be present during these birds' every waking hour:

> Oft frighted up they startle to the shade
> Of neighbouring wood and through the yellow leaves
> Drop wearied where the brakes and ferns hath made
> A solitary covert – that deceives
> For there the fox prowls its unnoticed round
> And danger dares them on every ground.

It might appear an obvious question, but if partridges are so vulnerable to predators – especially when breeding – why do they choose to nest on the ground in the first place? The reason goes back to the species' origins, on the treeless steppes of Central Asia. Having evolved to spend the vast majority of their lives on the ground, they are simply unable to change their habits to a more arboreal existence – notwithstanding that abiding image of 'a partridge in a pear tree'.

Nesting on the ground also makes partridges very vulnerable to the hazard of early mowing for silage or hay, in which whole clutches of eggs or broods of young chicks may be destroyed in a matter of moments. Heavy rain, too, is a hazard: a sudden downpour can rapidly chill eggs or chicks beyond the point of recovery.

It has long been known that when a partridge sitting on her nest is disturbed – whether deliberately or accidentally – she will follow the example of other ground-nesting birds and lure the intruder away by pretending to be injured or lame. The earliest writer on natural history, the Greek philosopher Aristotle, noted this fascinating behaviour in the fourth century BC:

> Partridges, when anyone comes near their nest, cast themselves down before his feet that looks for it, running and flying as if they were lame, by that means drawing him away from their nests, and enticing him to follow them; which when they have done, themselves fly away.

This strategy, known as a distraction or diversionary display, can be risky. If the bird ventures too close to the intruder, it may be caught or killed; but the trick must still work more often than not, or it would not have persisted. But not every sitting bird will flee, as Yarrell reported:

> A farmer discovered a Partridge sitting on its eggs in a grass-field. The bird allowed him to pass his hand frequently down its back without moving, or showing any fear: but if he offered to touch the eggs, the poor bird immediately pecked his hand.

When it comes to eggs, then, few British birds lay quite as many as the grey partridge – perhaps to compensate for the increased danger they face from nesting on the ground. A typical clutch consists of between thirteen and sixteen eggs, of an olive or greenish-grey shade, but as many as twenty-nine have been recorded – though this would have been from two or more females laying in the same nest. John Clare frequently came across larger-than-average clutches, described in his sonnet 'The Partridge's Nest':

> The partridge makes no nest but on the ground
> Lays many eggs and I have often found
> Sixteen or eighteen in a beaten seat
> When tracing o'er the fields or weeding wheat. . .

He also noted that, when weeding the fields, local boys would often raid the nests, and either use the eggs to play games with or take them home, presumably for food.

When the chicks are born, they are immediately ready to leave the nest; a behaviour termed 'precocial', which comes from the same root as the word 'precocious'. They cannot fly until they are about two weeks old, but are able to walk, run and hide from danger. The chicks can also feed themselves straight away, taking seeds and tiny insects, though they stay close to their parents for almost a year after hatching.

Partridges are both sedentary and sociable birds, forming small groups known as 'coveys', which means there are more birds to keep an eye out for predators. Staying low in long vegetation may help them remain unseen, but when that no longer works they will take flight in a whirr of wings, heading straight and low over to the other side of the field, then dropping down to the ground to hide once again. As they rise, they often utter their unique call: a rapid series of deep croaks. This sound has been compared with a key turning in a stiff lock, or a rusty gate swinging in the wind, but actually has a unique sonic quality that is hard to define in images or words.

In his *Ornithological Dictionary*, published in 1802, George Montagu noted the partridge's habit of gathering together in larger groups outside the breeding season: 'Sometimes three or four coveys will assemble in winter, and are then exceedingly shy. In vain may the sportsman pursue them.'

That last line reveals why this small, shy bird was so familiar to Montagu and his contemporaries. For the partridge is, like its relatives the pheasant and various species of grouse, one of a select handful of species defined as 'gamebirds': bred and released for shooting. Being so small, keeping hidden in the long vegetation at the edge of fields, and flying low when flushed, partridges are particularly renowned as providing 'good sport' for the pursuing marksman.

John Clare recalled that the beginning of shooting each autumn was often marked by the appearance of partridges in unexpected places:

> It is not a timid bird but on the shooting season is pursued with such unfeeling anxiety by the sportsman and his dogs that it seems to lose all fear in the confusion and will fly into a house . . . and suffer itself to be taken by the hand – one entered a house next door to mine last year and seemed as tame and as confident of protection as a chicken but the tenant being as heartless as the sportsmen it was killed and eaten . . .

The start of the partridge-shooting season was – and indeed still is – 1 September. This was jocularly referred to as 'St Partridge's Day', as in this comment from a character in the (then popular, but now long-forgotten) 1888 novel *Robert Elsmere* by Mrs Humphry Ward: 'Well, this *is* friendship! What on earth brings you here, old fellow? Why aren't you in the stubbles celebrating St. Partridge?'

The period during which this novel was written, from the late Victorian era to the eve of the First World War, was the heyday of partridge shooting. As Brian Vesey-Fitzgerald revealed, during a single day's shoot, at Holkham in Norfolk in 1905, no fewer than 1,671 birds were killed by just eight guns. Less than two decades earlier, in 1887, four days' shooting on a Hampshire estate yielded a grand total of 4,109 partridges. Given those figures, it is hard to imagine just how common the species must have been – suggestions that there would have been over one million breeding pairs in Britain as a whole seem credible.

Fate would provide a brief reprieve for the grey partridge. The start of the First World War in August 1914 meant that many of the men involved in shooting these birds were otherwise engaged. Ironically, the two groups in society who suffered the highest casualties in that terrible conflict were also those most involved in killing game: on the one hand, the aristocrats and landed gentry who actually shot the birds; on the other, the working-class gamekeepers and beaters who facilitated the sport. Both were, to say the least, good with firearms; both perhaps had a more exaggerated sense of duty than their urban counterparts; so it was only natural that they volunteered in their droves for what turned out to be a very different kind of slaughter, in the muddy fields of Flanders.

Perhaps the most poignant evocation of that last shooting season before the war, the autumn of 1913, appeared many years afterwards. *The Shooting Party* was a British-made film starring James Mason and Edward Fox, and also featuring Sir John Gielgud, Dorothy Tutin, Gordon Jackson and Robert Hardy in a stellar cast.

Based on the 1980 novel by Isabel Colegate, it tells of a gathering of English aristocrats and various hangers-on at a country estate, at which a competition to shoot the most gamebirds escalates into a bitter and ultimately tragic climax, when one over-competitive member of the group accidentally shoots one of the beaters dead.

The story is, of course, a parable about the coming slaughter in the trenches but, like an earlier novel, L. P. Hartley's *The Go-Between* (published in 1953 and also made into a film, in 1971), it highlights a very different world from that which came after the conflict.

Today, thanks to the sanitised *Downton Abbey* version, we may regard that period with longing and nostalgia, but Colegate and Hartley revealed the truth: that this was a strictly hierarchical, repressive and often very unpleasant society. Both used the killing of innocent birds as a metaphor for a wider contempt for human life.

Not that the temporary cessation of hostilities provided by the First (and later Second) World War made much difference to the long-term fate of this gamebird. During the inter-war period numbers stayed more or less stable, but the shift towards intensive agriculture during and after the Second World War was disastrous for all birds of the farmed countryside. In particular, the widespread reliance on chemical pesticides and herbicides, to control pests and kill weeds, spelled the death-knell for birds that depended on seeds to feed themselves and insects for their young – including, of course, the grey partridge.

In *The Vanishing Hedgerows*, a BBC documentary broadcast in 1973, the author and farmer Henry Williamson (of *Tarka the Otter* fame) spoke sorrowfully of the way that pesticides were killing his beloved birds. Williamson recalled finding a pair of partridges and their chicks on his Devon farm, 'crouched side by side in death, with their chicks slightly larger than humblebees, cold between the protective feathers'. By then the cause of the carnage in the countryside – the widespread misuse of chemicals such as DDT – had been shockingly exposed by Rachel Carson in her 1962 book *Silent Spring*.

Ironically, however, the one thing that saved the grey partridge from oblivion in some parts of Britain, notably East Anglia, was shooting. Because numbers of partridges have now dropped so low, and survival rates are still so poor, shooting estates now artificially breed and release young partridges, thus helping to maintain the population. And because no partridges means no profits, landowners have worked with tenant farmers to ensure that the use of pesticides and herbicides is kept to a minimum, and the habitat features the birds need, including a mix of different heights of vegetation, especially around the edges of fields, are provided.

Much of this positive land management is the result of one man's sheer hard work and vision. Dick Potts, who died in 2017 at the age of seventy-seven, was a Yorkshire farmer's son who became fascinated by partridges as a young child, after his father had given him a copy of Vesey-Fitzgerald's *British Game*. More than sixty-five years later, in 2012, Dick Potts made his own seminal contribution to the New Naturalist series with the 121st volume, entitled *Partridges: Countryside Barometer*.

Potts sets out his stall from the start, pointing out the inextricable links between farmland birds such as the partridge and our own likely fate:

This book is about far more than partridges. Mankind and partridges have evolved together, both ultimately dependent on

grasslands rather than forests. For thousands of years, both ate grass seeds, and this continued until cereals largely replaced them. Hundreds of species of plant and insect that partridges and other birds eat thrived on farms for thousands of years until the dawn of the pesticides era. Since then the long decline in partridge abundance has been a barometer for biodiversity over vast swathes of the Northern Hemisphere.

Throughout his working lifetime, Potts sought to discover why the grey partridge was undergoing such a steep decline. He identified what he called the 'three-legged stool': a reduction in the use of pesticides and herbicides, the provision of suitable nesting habitat, and the control of predators. If any one of these was missing, partridges would, he believed, inevitably disappear.

From 1968, by putting his theories into practice on the Duke of Norfolk's estate near Arundel in West Sussex, Potts and his colleagues managed to at least partially reverse the grey partridge's decline. In what became known as the 'Sussex Study', he also achieved a rare consensus between the often-opposed triumvirate of shooting, farming and conservation, who could all see the benefits of his ground-breaking approach.

He did so through the respect his matchless expertise commanded, and by his pragmatic methods. In the closing lines of his book he summed up the challenge ahead, and especially the need for the various lobby groups to work together to save this classic countryside species:

> I am absolutely convinced that a great deal of countryside biodiversity can be regained without compromising food production . . . It can only happen, however, if agribusiness, protectionist and hunter lobbies genuinely co-operate to solve the vexed issues. Too often these tribes play marbles in the middle of the road unaware of the juggernaut.

Dick Potts's achievements were widely recognised, and on the day of his death he was told he had won the RSPB's prestigious Gold Medal. Without him, it is fair to say, the plight of this very special rural bird would now be even more desperate.

*

The grey partridge was, until recently at least, a common, widespread and very familiar bird not just in Britain, but across much of temperate Europe and western and central Asia. Yet like so many other farmland birds it has suffered sharp declines over the past few decades just about everywhere: in the early 1950s the world population was estimated at about 100 million; today it is probably less than half that. The species has also been introduced to North America (for shooting, of course), where it is known as the Hungarian partridge, as the first birds came from eastern Europe.

Here in the UK it is sometimes still called the 'English' partridge, to distinguish it from its larger and more brightly-coloured relative the red-legged, or 'French' partridge. I recall the Norfolk farmer and conservationist Chris Knights once telling me that, when giving a talk in Scotland, he had inadvertently referred to the 'English partridge'. 'Buggers'll claim anything!' was the curt response.

The red-legged partridge was first introduced to Britain from continental Europe in the late seventeenth century, but it was not until a hundred years or so later that the birds were brought here on a large scale. They soon became popular: not only are they more adaptable and resilient than the greys, and easier to rear, but they are fatter too, and therefore more in demand as food. Today there are roughly twice as many red-legged as grey partridges in Britain and, being less shy, the species is far more likely to be seen than its native cousin – even, on occasion, coming into village gardens.

Because red-legged partridges do occasionally perch in trees, it has been suggested (by, amongst others, no less an authority than Mark Cocker) that the arboreal species in our Christmas carol may in fact be *Alectoris rufa*, the red-legged partridge. But that peculiar image of a 'partridge in a pear-tree', which has baffled so many people over the years, actually has a very simple and elegant solution, as revealed by Andrew Gant, a lecturer in music at St Peter's College, Oxford. It all comes down to a linguistic misunderstanding.

In his fascinating book *Christmas Carols: from Village Green to Church Choir*, Gant noted that the scientific name of the grey partridge is *Perdix perdix*. This originally came into English some time around the fourteenth century, via the Normans, from the Old French *pertriz*, which was later corrupted into the more English-sounding 'partridge'.

In modern French, however, the name of the species is *perdrix* – pronounced, of course, with a silent 'x' as 'pair-dree'. As Gant points out:

We have our pear tree. It's a *perdrix*. It's a half-remembered mis-translation, or, perhaps, a mis-remembered half-translation, giving us, oddly, not one partridge up a tree but two, both on the ground. One English, one French. A partridge *et un perdrix*.

Sorted. Or, as the French might say, *Voilà!*

Two Turtle Doves

TURTLE DOVES

A few years ago, when I was working at the BBC Natural History Unit in Bristol, a young researcher named Ruth Peacey greeted me one Monday morning with the words, 'Guess which bird I managed to twitch at Portland Bill this weekend!'

Given that it was May, at the height of the spring migration season, various possibilities went through my mind, from great spotted cuckoo to little bittern, and Alpine swift to bluethroat. I never for a moment imagined that this great rarity, which she had travelled so far to see, would be a species that, when I was her age, was a common summer visitor to southern England: the turtle dove.

Ruth is almost twenty-five years younger than me, so to her – and everyone else of her generation – the turtle dove is now a scarce and much sought-after bird. It does still breed in Britain: at the latest count, the British Trust for Ornithology (BTO) estimates that there are about 14,000 pairs, mostly in the drier counties of south-east England and East Anglia.

Fourteen thousand pairs may seem quite a lot, but this diminutive dove is on a downward spiral, rapidly hurtling towards oblivion. In just 25 years since 1994 – when I was Ruth's age –

its numbers have fallen by a staggering 93 per cent. Given that they were already starting to decline a few years earlier, it's likely that we have already lost nineteen out of twenty of the turtle doves that were breeding here in the 1980s. Currently, numbers are halving every six years. If this rate of decline continues – and there is no reason to suggest that it will not – the turtle dove will vanish as a British breeding bird sometime during the 2030s, and possibly even earlier.

The loss of any species is a tragedy, but the turtle dove's charm and beauty make its decline and likely disappearance even harder to bear. The species has always been a favourite amongst writers on birds, as this passage from J. E. Harting's 1875 book *Our Summer Migrants* reveals:

> Amidst the general harmony of the grove in spring, there are few prettier sounds than the gentle cooing of the Turtle-Dove . . . It pours forth its soft murmurings with a delightful *crescendo* and *diminuendo*, while close at hand, upon a mere frame-work of a nest, the mate sits brooding on her two milk-white eggs.

It was this 'gentle cooing' that gave the species its peculiar name, which, like so many of the names we give to birds, is a corruption of the original version. 'Turtle' has absolutely nothing to do with the familiar aquatic reptile, but is a representation of the soft, somnolent and repetitive '*tur-tur*' call given by the male dove during the late spring and summer. It's not only the English name that reflects this: no fewer than thirteen other European languages also include the bird's sound into their name for the

Dove

turtle dove: from the Welsh *turtur* to the French *tourterelle de bois*, and the Dutch *zomertortel*, to the wonderfully tongue-twisting Finnish version, *turturikyyhky*.

With the possible exception of the cuckoo, few sounds better conjure up the long, hot and lazy days of midsummer than the call of the turtle dove. This makes it even more shocking that this timeless sound can no longer be heard across large swathes of the species' former range.

More than twenty years ago, when I regularly watched birds at Lonsdale Road Reservoir, alongside the banks of the River Thames in south-west London, I noticed a smaller bird with a flock of woodpigeons, feeding on the adjacent school playing field. Lifting my binoculars, I was surprised to see a turtle dove: even in those days this was an increasingly scarce bird, especially in the capital. Little was I to know that this would be the last time I would see a turtle dove on any of my local patches.

When I moved to Somerset, just over a decade ago, I assumed that I would enjoy hearing the call of the turtle dove in and around my new home. But I simply hadn't registered the trouble the bird was already in: not only have I never seen or heard a turtle dove in Somerset, but I suspect I never shall.

Once so common that observers didn't even bother to send in records of the species, by the turn of the millennium it had disappeared as a breeding bird from the county. A calling dove was heard in the Brendon Hills in 2008, and two migrants were observed there in August 2010; but in 2011, for the first time since records began, not a single turtle dove was recorded in Somerset.

The turtle dove is the perfect example of Shifting Baseline Syndrome, a concept first developed half a century ago, which draws attention to the way each new generation assumes that what they witness is the norm. This has profound implications for the conservation of birds and other wildlife: if you assume, from your own experience, that a species has always been as common or rare as it is today, then you will fail to appreciate the rapid and sometimes catastrophic shifts in status and numbers that are occurring over a period of time.

It works both ways, of course. We now live in a world where buzzards and little egrets are commonplace, whereas, when I began birding, half a century ago, they were incredibly rare. Likewise, as we have seen, in my childhood grey partridges and, to a lesser extent, turtle doves, were common, whereas now they are on the brink of extinction in Britain.

*

For those of us who still recall seeing turtle doves, and younger readers who may never have had that privilege, it is worth dwelling a while on their appearance and habits.

The turtle dove is by far the smallest member of its family in Britain: far tinier than the plump and familiar woodpigeon, stock dove and feral pigeon, and also noticeably smaller than a bird whose fortunes could hardly have been more different over the past few decades, the collared dove. At just 27 centimetres (11 inches) long, and weighing only 140 grams (less than five ounces), the turtle dove is only marginally larger than a black-bird, and less than one-third of the weight of a woodpigeon.

Its small size and slender build give it a delicate quality compared with its larger, bulkier cousins, like a ballet dancer mingling with a group of rugby players. The bird's beauty is enhanced by its plumage: the back and upperwings are scalloped with an orange and dark grey tortoiseshell pattern, offset by a delicate pinkish-purple wash on the face, neck and breast, shading to pale buffy-white on the belly, an ash-grey crown, orange eye, and a patch of narrow, black-and-white stripes on the side of the neck.

In flight, the bird reveals dark grey wing-feathers and a distinctive tail pattern: the dark grey and black centre of the noticeably wedge-shaped tail is fringed with broad bands of white on the outer feathers. The overall effect is like a delicate oriental sculpture, enhanced by the bird's graceful bearing.

Even when the turtle dove was far commoner in Britain, it was always one of the latest birds to arrive back from Africa, usually reaching our shores in the last week of April or the first week of May. In Somerset, the mean arrival date from 1926 to 1991 was

2 May, with the earliest sighting on 12 April, a pattern mirrored elsewhere in southern England. The long wait before they returned was summed up by the Victorian ornithologist William Yarrell in this bittersweet tribute: 'Their appearance is observed and hailed with pleasure each returning spring, as denoting the season of buds and flowers, and as emblems of serenity and peace their mournfully plaintive notes give pleasure.'

Once turtle doves return, they soon get down to the serious business of courtship and mating. Like other pigeons and doves, the male tentatively approaches the female and tries to win her over by strutting around, puffing out his chest, nodding his head and uttering soft purring sounds. She usually feigns indifference, to test his fidelity and persistence. He may also do a courtship flight, making parabolic arcs in the air as he flies up and down, occasionally cracking his wings like a whip to attract her attention. Eventually, if she likes what she sees – and hears – they will pair up, mate and begin the process of raising a family.

For such a neat, dapper bird, the turtle dove's nest is a surprisingly messy and slapdash construction. It is a flimsy assemblage of twigs and the stalks of plants, lined with a few pieces of grass, and usually placed a few feet up in a hawthorn, elder, or other hedgerow shrub. Having mated, the female will lay two pure white eggs, with a smooth and glossy surface, which she incubates for about two weeks. The young, which like other pigeon and dove chicks are born helpless, blind and naked apart from a few downy feathers, fledge after another three weeks, though they may leave the nest a few days earlier.

Traditionally, doves – and more especially turtle doves – are regarded as symbols of monogamy and fidelity. This goes right back to the Ancient Greeks, who regarded the dove (usually a white one) as the symbol of the goddess of love Aphrodite (to the Romans, Venus), who was often accompanied by doves either flying around her or perched on her hand. There is a ring of truth to this: unlike many other birds, which are serially unfaithful to their primary partners, doves do tend to stay faithful to the same mate through the whole breeding season, and sometimes also from year to year.

Crucial questions to answer are when – and especially why – did the decline of the turtle dove begin? The first BTO *Atlas of Breeding Birds*, published in 1976 and based on five years' fieldwork from 1968 to 1972, still paints a rather rosy picture of the species' fortunes, noting that there has been 'a steady increase from 1962 to the present'.

If we go back further still, during the nineteenth century the turtle dove increased both in numbers and range, thanks to new methods of arable farming, which produced plenty of seeds throughout the spring and summer months. During the second half of Queen Victoria's reign, the species expanded northwards and westwards from its earlier strongholds in East Anglia and the south-east, reaching Wales, Yorkshire and Cumberland (now Cumbria). Numbers then plateaued in the early decades of the twentieth century, following which they began to rise again, with the turtle dove reaching the Scottish borders in the years following the Second World War.

By the time of the 1968-72 *Atlas* survey, the UK population was thought to be as many as 125,000 pairs: more than the stock dove, and over three times as many as the collared dove. Today, that situation has massively reversed: with roughly one million pairs, the collared dove is now seventy times commoner than its smaller cousin.

So unlike, say, the decline of the red-backed shrike and wryneck – two other once common birds now no longer breeding in Britain – which began before the Second World War and accelerated rapidly afterwards, turtle doves appear to have been more or less OK until sometime during the 1980s. By the end of that decade, however, numbers had almost halved, to around 75,000 pairs, making the species a new candidate for the Red List of endangered and vulnerable birds.

At the time, the fall in numbers was seen as linked to the increased prevalence of droughts in the Sahel Zone of sub-Saharan Africa, where many British turtle doves spend up to two-thirds of their lives. Other species known to overwinter in West Africa, including the sand martin and whitethroat, were also suffering sudden, rapid and unexpected declines, and so this explanation made sense.

But, as we were soon to discover, what was happening in the turtle dove's winter-quarters was only part of the story. Events at home, when the doves arrived back after their 5,600-km (3,500-mile) journey, were also a key influence on their fortunes. In 2005, a study showed that changes in the way arable farmland was being managed – notably the loss of tall, dense hedgerows where the doves nest, and the lack of weed seeds on which they feed – were another major problem.

Turtle doves feed themselves and their young exclusively on the seeds of arable weeds such as fumitory, which has virtually been wiped out from large areas of lowland Britain as farmers seek to maximise their yields of wheat and barley. Because the birds cannot get enough food throughout the breeding season, they are now no longer managing to produce a second brood of young. As a result, they are only raising half as many chicks as they did in the 1970s, so their productivity is dropping like a stone. Put simply, if a species cannot raise enough young to sustain its numbers, it will start to decline, and eventually disappear.

As if all that were not bad enough, turtle doves also suffer from climate change, which is allowing the plants that do provide seeds to bloom earlier in the spring. But turtle doves are still arriving back in Britain at the same time every year, by which time the seeds they need to eat have already been and gone: the birds are unable to adapt quickly enough to deal with these very rapid changes in the seasons. A further factor is that turtle doves appear to be very vulnerable to the parasitic disease trichomonosis, which has already devastated our greenfinch population.

Finally, there is the problem facing the doves as they cross the Mediterranean on their journey south in autumn and back northwards in spring: indiscriminate slaughter by shooting. This is especially bad in the eastern Mediterranean, on islands such as Malta, but also occurs throughout much of France, Spain and Italy. Turtle doves migrate by day and, although they are fast, they also tend to fly in a straight line, making them easy to pick out and shoot as they pass by.

This has been brought to public attention by some brave and committed people in Malta, such as the conservationist Joe Sultana, and more recently by a team of filmmakers led by the wildlife TV presenter Chris Packham and Ruth Peacey herself. At great danger to themselves, Ruth and her team have produced a number of short films, aired on YouTube and publicised using social media, which have drawn attention to the plight of turtle doves and other migrant birds as they cross the island each spring and autumn.

*

Faced with the evidence about the problems faced by the turtle dove, and its recent devastating decline, it is tempting to give up the species as a lost cause. But fortunately, many people cannot face that prospect, and so have banded together to try to save it.

Operation Turtle Dove is a partnership of four organisations – the RSPB, Natural England, the Pensthorpe Conservation Trust and the wildlife-friendly farming scheme Fair to Nature – which is using practical methods, based on the latest scientific research, to help bring the turtle dove back from the brink. The group has been working closely with farmers to offer advice and help in managing their land for turtle doves, including obtaining Countryside Stewardship grants to help them do so. Early indications are that this is beginning to work, at least on the local level.

This far-sighted, holistic approach, which deals with the threats facing the species both at home and abroad, is a fine example of how to help a species whose lifestyle crosses so many borders and touches such a wide range of people. Whether it will ultimately work, or if, as many people fear, it is too late to save this emblematic farmland species, is still uncertain. But at least they are trying.

One reason why people are so passionate about the turtle dove is the species' central part in our folklore and culture. Given that (discounting the collared dove, which first colonised Britain in the 1950s) it has always been the least widespread of our pigeons and doves, this may strike us as odd. But one explanation is that turtle doves have always been seen as a symbol of love and fidelity, because the birds are often seen in pairs, huddled up against one another like human lovers. Whether turtle doves are actually monogamous is arguable, but the point is that we have long regarded them to be so. And as much of our literature revolves around notions of faithfulness, the turtle dove has, down the ages, been the perfect symbol.

This has been so for a very long time: our deep cultural attachment to the turtle dove goes back almost to the dawn of civilisation. In the Old Testament book 'The Song of Solomon', surely the most poetic in the Bible, the following lines describe the coming of spring to the Holy Land:

> For lo, the winter is past, the rain is over and gone. The flowers appear on the earth; the time of the singing of birds is come, and the voice of the turtle is heard in our land . . .

Later versions, for the sake of clarity, change 'turtle' to 'turtle dove(s)', to make it clear that the verse does not refer to singing aquatic reptiles. One of these, the English Standard Version, was heard by a television audience of millions when, at Prince Harry and Meghan Markle's wedding in May 2018, it was read by Lady Jane Fellowes, Princess Diana's elder sister and Harry's aunt.

The cultural impact of this single Biblical verse cannot be overestimated. It has – perhaps uniquely – given rise to no fewer than three works of literature: Elizabeth Chadwick's historical tale *The Time of Singing* (promoted as 'a testament to the power of sacrifice and the strength of love'), Richard Powers' literary novel *The Time of Our Singing* (a tale of how two brothers overcome prejudice through making music) and a romantic comedy play and film by John William Van Druten, both produced in the 1940s, *The Voice of the Turtle*.

The anonymous author (or authors) of 'The Song of Solomon', which was written some time between the tenth and second centuries BC, would have been very familiar with the spring migration of the turtle dove. Even today, tens of thousands of these birds still pass through the Middle East on their twice-yearly journeys to and from Europe and Africa. Indeed, of all the world's 300 or so pigeons and doves, the turtle dove undertakes by far the longest migratory voyage: a round trip of over 11,000 km (6,900 miles).

Other ancient Mediterranean cultures also featured many references to the bird. Aphrodite, the Greek goddess of love, had her chariot pulled through the skies by a pair of turtle doves, while Fides, the Roman goddess of trust and good faith, was usually portrayed holding a turtle dove in her hands. Aristotle (translated in the sixteenth century by William Turner) pronounced that 'the smallest [dove] is the Turtur' (a clear reference to the onomatopoeic origin of the bird's name). But, being largely unaware of the process of migration, he also noted that 'in the winter [the turtle dove] lies hid, for it conceals itself at the due time.'

One of the most intriguing appearances of the species is in a portrait of Giuliano de' Medici, the fifteenth-century ruler of Florence and a great patron of the arts, who was assassinated by rivals in April 1478, aged just twenty-five, but immortalised by the artist Sandro Botticelli just before his untimely death.

The young man is depicted, eyes half-closed, wearing a crimson gown, as he stands by an open window. The only other feature in the painting is a bird – unmistakably a turtle dove – which perches by his right arm, gazing in the opposite direction to the sitter. According to scholars of early Renaissance iconography, the bird is a symbol of loyalty; in this case to de' Medici's courtly love Simonetta Vespucci, who had recently died.

Chaucer – one of the most bird-obsessed of all our writers – also used the turtle dove as a symbol of love and fidelity, a belief going back to classical times. In *The Parlement of Foules* he wrote of 'the wedded turtle with hir herte trewe'; a theme later taken up by Shakespeare, in his love-poem 'The Phoenix and the Turtle'. Shakespeare also featured the turtle dove in no fewer than five of his plays, including (in *The Merry Wives of Windsor*) in a line that might appeal to the modern birder: 'We'll teach him to know turtles from jays . . .'

Shakespeare's fellow-poet, the soldier and courtier Sir Philip Sidney, also praised the bird as a symbol of fidelity over time:

> Time will work what no man knoweth
> Time doth us the subject prove
> With time still affection groweth
> To the faithful turtle dove.

Later writers who referred to the turtle dove are as varied as Edgar Allen Poe and Anne Brontë, Nikolai Gogol and Carol Ann Duffy. The Poe reference is especially striking, given that it focuses on a turtle dove listening to the romantic sound of wedding bells, very different from his usual Gothic horror. The species also features in the songs of Cliff Richard (the 1962 hit 'Bachelor

Boy'), Annie Lennox (the 1992 song 'Precious') and even Frank Sinatra ('The Look of Love'). However, as the Operation Turtle Dove website notes, this may simply be because 'dove' conveniently rhymes with 'love'. They go on to point out that 'turtle' is Cockney rhyming slang for 'love' (and, rather less romantically, 'glove').

But it cannot be doubted that, from Old Testament prophets to poets and singers to songwriters, we have long celebrated the supposed monogamy of the turtle dove.

Yet if we think of turtle doves today, the most powerful images are not the perennial symbols of love and fidelity, or even the purring summer sound of a cooing male in the English countryside, but the relentless crack of shotguns, followed by the birds falling dead or wounded from the sky, over the Mediterranean island of Malta.

Astonishingly, on Malta, two species can still be legally shot during their migration: the quail and the turtle dove. With both species in decline, it seems bizarre that shooting them (unlike all the other birds) is, for the time being at least, legal, with a quota of 5,000 turtle doves permitted to be shot each spring. In fact, the number killed far exceeds this. Turtle doves have always been caught to eat: murals from Ancient Egypt portray birds that are unmistakably of this species being trapped using nets. But today no-one needs the birds for food: they are simply being massacred out of some misguided sense of fun.

This annual massacre – defended as traditional, even though the birds are no longer hunted for food – is not some minor issue: it has been estimated that, of the turtle dove's European population, which after the breeding season (with 3 to 6 million breeding pairs producing an average of 1 to 2 young) ranges from nine to twenty-four million birds, between two and three million are shot every year. That's anything between one in twelve and one in three turtle doves being killed. No wonder the decline in the UK has also been mirrored across the rest of Europe, with four out of five turtle doves having vanished since 1980. In 2015, following pressure from the European Union, the Maltese held a referendum on spring hunting: the vote to continue the practice passed with a majority of just 2,200 out of a total of more than 250,000 votes cast – less than one per cent.

In his book *A Message from Martha*, the author and conservationist Mark Avery tells the tragic story of the passenger pigeon, once the most numerous species of bird in the world, whose vast flocks darkened the skies of North America for hours on end as they passed overhead. Yet within just fifty years, by 1914, the species was extinct; lost through a combination of hunting and habitat loss. Having told his tale, Mark draws a chilling parallel with the rapid decline of the turtle dove during the past few decades; a decline that has led the RSPB to describe the species as 'Europe's Passenger Pigeon'.

If the turtle dove does go the way of the passenger pigeon, the great auk and the dodo, then its iconography will have changed forever. For it will no longer be a symbol of love, loyalty and fidelity, but of our own misplaced belief that we can exploit the planet's resources with absolutely no consequences. Its plight also represents the triumph of ruthlessness and indifference, the very opposite of those qualities we associate with the turtle dove. And we will never again be able to sing the second line of our best-known Christmas carol, without thinking of the disappearance of this beautiful bird.

POSTSCRIPT

Just as this book was going to print, the Rare Breeding Birds Panel made this shock announcement: 'Following steep declines, it is now believed that there are fewer than 2,000 breeding pairs [of turtle doves] in the UK.' If true, this charismatic species is likely to disappear from our countryside within the next decade.

Three French Hens

DOMESTIC CHICKENS

Deep in the jungles of northern India, an hour or so before dawn, a bird begins to stir. It emerges from its night-time roost in the dense undergrowth and flies up into the lower branches of a tree. Moments later, the bird, a male red junglefowl, proclaims the imminent arrival of daybreak with a loud, far-carrying call. It's a sound that, even if you have never seen or heard this species before, is very familiar. *'Cock-a-doodle doooooo!'*

Hundreds of miles away, in the Indian capital of New Delhi, workers are arriving at the Ambience Mall, whose slogan proclaims it to be a 'space for a million smiles'. Some are heading for the mall's boutiques, while others clock on at its many fast-food restaurants. Amongst these, you may not be surprised to discover, is one offering 'Finger-lickin' chicken at affordable rates . . .' Its name? KFC.

KFC – still known to older customers by its original name, 'Kentucky Fried Chicken' – is one of the most successful fast food franchises in the world. Based on the number of global locations it comes in fourth place, behind Subway, McDonald's and Starbucks, with over 20,000 outlets producing an annual revenue of $23 billion. Not bad for a brand whose origins are indeed in the eponymous US state of Kentucky, having been founded by 'Colonel' Harland Sanders. He started his career selling fried chicken in a roadside restaurant on the edge of the Appalachian Mountains during the Great Depression, and ended up a multi-millionaire.

The connection between the elusive bird crowing at dawn in the Himalayan foothills and the fast-food outlet in the Delhi shopping mall may not be immediately obvious. But the link is a long-standing one: for the red junglefowl is the ancestor of the bird now being consumed by the billion in homes, cafés, canteens, fast-food joints and exclusive restaurants all over the world – the domestic chicken.

How this shy and rather obscure member of the pheasant family became the staple diet of so many of the world's people is a tale that at times seems stranger than fiction. It began at least 7,400 years ago, in a province in the north-east of China. Here, a group of Neolithic settlers known as the 'Cishan' (or 'Chishan') people began to capture the wild red junglefowl (*Gallus gallus*) that lived in the forests around their homes, and keep the birds in captivity.

Ironically, given how much we now rely on the chicken for food, in the form of meat and eggs, this early domestication may actually have been for a very different reason. Male red junglefowl frequently fight their rivals – indeed, they have evolved a sharp spur on the rear of their legs for just this purpose. There is some evidence to suggest that the junglefowl was first domesticated for 'sport': the cruel, brutal activity that has come to be known as 'cockfighting'. But it cannot have been long before the

bird's other qualities – plump, firm flesh, abundant feathers and the propensity to lay plenty of tasty and nutritious eggs – were also appreciated.

The same process of catching birds in the wild, and then breeding them for whichever qualities were desired, was soon taking place in other civilisations elsewhere in Asia. By roughly 5000 BC, only a few centuries after the Chinese had first domesticated the red junglefowl, people in the Ganges region of north-eastern India were doing the same, as were those in the Indus Valley in north-western India and Pakistan. At some point, they may also have captured the closely-related grey junglefowl, as the latest genetic studies of chickens suggest that the yellow skin of the domestic bird may originate from this species, which may have interbred with the descendants of the red junglefowl.

The red and grey junglefowls – along with the two other members of their genus, the Sri Lanka junglefowl and the green junglefowl of Indonesia – are from the large and varied family Phasianidae. This comprises more than 180 species of gamebird, including pheasants, partridges, quails, francolins, grouse, turkey and peafowl. Other members, such as the common pheasant and grey and red-legged partridges, have been semi-domesticated to be bred, released and shot, while the wild turkey of the Americas is the ancestor of the bird we eat at Christmas. But why, of all these plump, tasty and relatively easy-to-catch birds, was the red junglefowl the one domesticated first?

The reason appears to be connected with the peculiar breeding biology of this species. It evolved to take advantage of the glut of seeds released by bamboo plants at the end of their long seeding cycle, when females will respond to the greater availability of food by laying a clutch of eggs, whatever the time of year.

When the species was domesticated, its owners soon discovered that, given enough food, the birds would respond by laying more eggs. By then selecting the best layers and breeding from them, they ended up with a bird that can produce up to 300 eggs in a single year (the authenticated record is an incredible 371 eggs in 364 days). Compared to the usual number laid in the wild – between 10 and 15 eggs a year – that's quite an achievement.

Once these early civilisations discovered the advantages of keeping chickens, the practice spread like wildfire, following the trade routes east and west. By 3000 BC, chickens had reached south-east Europe, yet it took another 2,000 years for them to arrive in western Europe, via the Phoenicians, and later the Romans. They also went the other way around the world, crossing the vast Pacific Ocean (possibly with Polynesian explorers) to reach the Americas, perhaps even before Europeans conquered the New World.

Whichever way chickens managed to spread around the globe, they have become not only the commonest and most successful domestic bird, but also by far the most numerous bird on the planet. The statistics are simply mindboggling: the latest figures from the United Nations' Food and Agriculture Organisation (FAO) suggest that the total number of chickens alive at any one time is about 19 *billion* – that's more than two chickens for every human being. To put this figure into perspective, the commonest wild bird in the world, the tiny red-billed quelea of sub-Saharan Africa, numbers roughly 1.5 billion breeding pairs.

Watching a red junglefowl in the forests of Northern India, as I first did more than thirty years ago, I remember being forcefully struck by its close resemblance to our own domestic chickens, especially when it comes to the male.

The male junglefowl is one of the most colourful birds in the world. However, because he spends so much of his life in the understorey beneath the thick forest canopy, where the different shades of his plumage merge together to provide camouflage, his beauty is only truly revealed when he momentarily emerges into a sunlit clearing. Then, you are dazzled by his rich combination of colours: an orange shawl across his shoulders; overlapping layers of magenta, teal and russet feathers; a long, plumed tail in a deep Prussian blue; all topped off with his bright red face, head, wattle and coxcomb. As he walks in and out of the dappled sunlight, his tail glimmers with iridescence, with flashes of blue, green and purple as it catches the rays of light.

The female is, as you would expect from this ground-nesting bird, far less striking than her mate: she looks rather like a fran-

colin (partridge-like members of the same family), and from a distance appears mainly a rather dull greyish-brown. However, as with other female gamebirds, a closer look reveals a subtle beauty, with shades of orange and streaks of black and white across her plumage. Her drabber, more cryptic appearance is, of course, a defence against predators; for like other members of this family, she alone incubates the eggs and looks after the chicks once they have hatched.

But it is these birds' behaviour that really seems familiar. In the wild, junglefowl usually live in groups ruled by the dominant male, with a few subordinate males and the females. During the breeding season, male red junglefowl welcome the coming of the new day in the way familiar to anyone who has ever kept chickens, or just spent the night in the countryside: the ear-splittingly loud, and utterly unmistakable, 'cock's crow'.

As with any regular sound made by male birds while breeding, this serves a dual purpose. It alerts rival males that the caller has survived the night, and is still in possession of his territory, and it signals to any potential mates – and this species is polygynous, breeding with several females – that he is ready for action.

The sound is, it seems, far more important than that bright and attractive plumage. Studies have revealed that females are initially attracted to males by their sound; then, once they have seen them, they prefer males with large coxcombs on their head. Oddly, perhaps, the brightness of the cockerels' plumage does not appear to influence their choice.

Sound is also crucial in warning other junglefowl of the presence of predators; indeed, this factor also plays a part in mate selection amongst females. The male produces distinctly different calls, depending on whether the threat comes from an aerial predator such as an eagle or hawk, or a ground-based one such as a tiger, leopard, or smaller species of wild cat. This is vital to the birds' survival: red junglefowl spend most of their lives on the forest floor, making them very vulnerable; only at sunset do they take to the wing, flying the short distance up into a tree where they will roost for the night.

When actively feeding, which they mainly do around dawn and dusk, both the male and his females will scratch around on the ground with their feet, in much the same way domestic cocks and hens do. When the male does find food, he often performs a distinctive display: moving his head and neck jerkily backwards and forwards, while making clucking sounds. He will sometimes pick up a morsel of food and then drop it, to entice his mate either to pick it up for herself or take it directly from his bill.

This is not just about food, but sex too. Having shown his commitment to her by offering her something to eat, he often subsequently mates with her, in the junglefowl equivalent of giving a box of chocolates in the hope of a successful seduction later on. Like other members of their large family, junglefowl mainly feed on fruits and seeds, but will also take insects and other invertebrates when they come across them. On occasion they will take larger items of prey, such as lizards, rodents and even small snakes.

Male domestic roosters – at least in their classic form – share their wild ancestor's brightly coloured plumage, long, flowing tail, and comb and wattle on the head. And, like their wild counterparts, female chickens are usually much smaller and drabber than the males, with a less ornate plumage.

Because domestic birds have been bred into so many different varieties – at the latest count, more than 500 worldwide – many breeds no longer even vaguely resemble their wild cousins. However, when it comes to behaviour, they have retained many wild traits.

Domestic chickens, like junglefowl, are sociable birds, which prefer to live in small groups or flocks. To keep order amongst them, both males and females adhere to a strict 'pecking order', in which some birds are dominant over others. These birds get first access to food, and the best locations to nest and lay their eggs.

During the years when we kept our own chickens, when my children were young, we were advised to have a cockerel 'to keep the hens in check'. Elvis, a splendid bottle-green Sumatran rooster, managed to do so until most of his hens were killed by a rogue fox that had somehow breached our electric fence. After this, he took to moping around in the bike shed, leaving his messy white droppings on our bicycles, until one dark night he suffered the same fate as his harem.

Elvis did not attempt to breed with his hens – or if he tried, we didn't notice – but when courting, as with other kinds of behaviour, domestic chickens follow very similar patterns to their wild ancestors. As in most relationships in the bird world, events are initiated by the male, which approaches the hen and tests her receptivity to his advances. The male and female perform a series of carefully co-ordinated displays, including her crouching in a submissive position while he moves around her in what is called 'the circle dance'. During this period, he also utters various calls. Finally, when he judges the time to be right, he mounts her and mates.

She will then find a safe place to lay her eggs. If left to her own devices, she would wait until she had a full clutch of about a dozen, and then incubate them until the chicks are ready to hatch. In captivity, however, hens do not get the chance to follow these natural instincts, as their owners remove each egg soon after it has been laid.

If a clutch of fertilised eggs does get incubated, the chicks hatch out after about three weeks. When ready to emerge, the chick will make a high-pitched '*peeping*' sound, to which the hen responds with a series of encouraging clucks. Instinctively, the chick then uses its 'egg tooth' – a sharp protuberance on its bill, which is shed soon after hatching – to break a tiny hole in the egg's shell, which over time it gradually enlarges until the shell cracks and it can emerge.

Like other species in its family, both junglefowl and domestic chicks are 'precocial', so they are able to see, walk, feed and fend for themselves almost immediately after hatching, though the hen will guard them carefully for several weeks afterwards. In doing so, she may change from what the eighteenth-century ornithologist Thomas Bewick called her 'state of continual joy' when incubating her eggs, into a staunch defender of her tiny and vulnerable offspring: 'From being the most . . . timid of birds, she becomes impatient, anxious, and fearless, attacking every animal, however fierce or powerful, that but seems to threaten her tender brood.'

After the chick has hatched, the 'egg tooth' soon disappears, but sometimes chickens can develop what appear to be embryonic versions of real teeth. For centuries the phrase 'as rare as hens' teeth' was used to describe something impossible – rather like 'pigs might fly'. Yet in 2006 this notion was turned on its head, when scientists in a joint UK-US team managed to stimulate chickens to produce natural teeth. It turns out that the (very) distant ancestors of domestic chickens (and, presumably, red junglefowl), did produce teeth, and that, 80 million years on, modern birds still retain the ability to do so.

*

Cock

Chickens – and their wild ancestors – have a long and varied place in our mythology, history and high and popular culture. Their early domestication inevitably led to them being used in religious ceremonies, sometimes as a sacrificial victim. However, perhaps because in many cultures – including Ancient Greece – the chicken was still a rare creature, used as food only for special ceremonies, it was often considered taboo to kill a chicken in such a way.

The bravery of the cockerel was also celebrated: it features in several of *Aesop's Fables*, written in Greece around the sixth century BC. These include 'The Cock and the Fox', in which a cockerel manages to outwit his mortal enemy, and 'The Lion, the Rooster and the Donkey', in which the mighty King of Beasts shows an irrational fear of the rooster.

From Aesop onwards, chickens appear in a wide range of other literary works. These include George Orwell's *Animal Farm*, in which the hens lead a rebellion when Napoleon, the pig who represents the tyrant Stalin, demands that their eggs be taken away for sale. The consequences for the rebellious chickens are fatal: having flown up to the rafters of the barn to lay their eggs, which fall down on to the floor and smash to pieces, they then find that the other animals are forbidden to give them food, so they starve to death.

Cockerels also feature in Hindu, Chinese and Jewish cultures, but perhaps the most famous cultural reference comes in the New Testament, where Jesus tells his disciple Peter that he will betray him three times 'before the cock crow . . .', a prophesy that, despite Peter's repeated denials, does indeed come to pass, in Mark, Chapter 14 Verse 72:

> And the second time the cock crew. And Peter called to mind the word that Jesus said unto him, Before the cock crow twice, thou shalt deny me thrice. And when he thought thereon, he wept.

Later, the sixth-century Pope Gregory I pronounced that the cockerel was a symbol of Christianity, and an image of the bird was placed on the steeples of churches. It is also the emblem of the North London football club Tottenham Hotspur, a connection that arose because the club was named after the late medieval nobleman Sir Henry (Harry) Hotspur, who kept fighting cocks fitted with spurs.

But cockerels – or cockerel-like creatures – had a darker side, too. The mythological cockatrice figured strongly in Tudor culture: a bizarre, two-legged creature with the body of a snake, the wings of a dragon and the head of a cockerel, which could kill people simply by looking at them. The cockatrice, which was supposedly hatched from a cock's egg, appears in a range of works from the late-fourteenth through to the sixteenth centuries, including the King James Bible, the poetry of Edmund Spenser and, most famously, in Shakespeare's *Romeo and Juliet*, when Juliet refers to 'the death-darting eye of cockatrice'.

A more conventional – yet also rather malevolent – cockerel appears in the seventeenth century poet Sir Charles Sedley's short verse 'On a Cock at Rochester', which takes the form of a wonderfully choleric diatribe against being woken early by the crowing of a rooster:

> Thou cursed Cock, with thy perpetual Noise
> May'st thou be Capon made, and lose thy Voice,
> Or on a Dunghill may'st thou spend thy Blood,
> And Vermin prey upon thy craven Brood;
> May Rivals tread thy Hens before thy Face,
> Then with redoubled Courage give thee chase;
> May'st thou be punish'd for St. Peter's Crime,
> And on Shrove-Tuesday, perish in thy Prime;
> May thy bruis'd Carcass be some Beggar's Feast,
> Thou first and worst Disturber of Man's Rest.

The domestic chicken is also, of course, the same species as the 'three French hens' that appear in our Christmas carol. But what exactly is a 'French hen'? Some commentators have suggested that the verse arises from the link between the scientific name of the chicken (and red junglefowl) *Gallus gallus*, and the Latin word for France, 'Gaul'. The rooster has always been a symbol connected with France: from the Gallic rooster of the French Revolution to the logo of the sportswear firm Le Coq Sportif.

What is perhaps more likely is that French breeds of hen (of which there are more than fifty different varieties) have always been prized for their tasty flesh. Indeed, one breed, *Bresse Gauloise*, was famously called 'the queen of poultry and the poultry of kings' by the early nineteenth-century gastronome Jean Anthelme Brillat-Savarin (who also gave his name to a variety of creamy, white soft cheese, created in homage to his memory). *Poulet de Bresse*, famous for its firm, white meat, continues to be produced under strict conditions in the Bresse region of eastern France.

Chickens also feature in popular culture – so much so that in May 2002 Yale University hosted a three-day conference on 'The Chicken: Its Biological, Social, Cultural and Industrial History from the Middle Ages to McNuggets'. This brought together 'scholars, agronomists, chicken growers, industry representatives and activists from the labor, farm, animal welfare, environmental and public health movements, who have studied the economic, social, health and ecological consequences of poultry rearing from past to present'. The event also included poetry readings, a film festival and cookery demonstrations (featuring both real chickens and vegetarian chicken substitutes).

No doubt the delegates to the Yale conference found it hard to resist telling what may be the world's most frequently told joke:

> Why did the chicken cross the road?
> To get to the other side.

As has been solemnly pointed out, this is an early example of an 'anti-joke', in which the expected punchline is subverted by a statement of the obvious. Perhaps that explains why this joke, which first appeared in a New York magazine in 1847, has given rise to so many different variations, which employ painful puns, alternative animals and the occasional surrealist version. However, as the writer and critic Matthew Sweet wryly observed in a

2004 feature on the cultural history of the chicken, nobody has yet come up with an amusing punchline. Sweet also unearthed a much earlier, and sexually explicit, chicken joke, based on the supposed resemblance of the erect male member to a posturing cockerel, written by an anonymous poet in the fifteenth century:

> I Have a Gentil Cock,
> Croweth me day
> He doth me risen early
> My matins for to say.

The other famous chicken 'joke' – or perhaps that should be 'riddle', is 'Which came first – the chicken or the egg?' This apparently insoluble paradox has recently been solved by scientists, who argue that the chicken descended from chicken-like ancestors (which they call 'proto-chickens'), but which were not actually chickens. However, when two of these mated and the female laid an egg, their genetic combination in the embryo mutated into a new species: the chicken. So logically, the egg came first.

In recent years, the way we exploit domestic chickens has come under increased scrutiny. Every hour of every day, in the United States alone, almost one million chickens are slaughtered for food: a grand total of eight billion each year. Overall, roughly fifty billion chickens are raised worldwide each year for eggs or meat. The vast majority of these – about three-quarters of those raised for meat and over two-thirds of those bred for eggs – are kept in 'factory farms'. They exist in conditions where they have very little space to move, giving rise to concerns for animal rights, and also for the potentially adverse effects on our own health and well-being.

The arguments against factory farming are perhaps not as clear-cut as many advocates for free-range alternatives suggest. One problematic issue is that free-range birds take up far more space, which means that more land is needed, which creates its own environmental problems. But increasingly, consumer demand is pushing the producers to reconsider their methods.

Perhaps we need to return to a time when, as my aunt (now in her late eighties) recalls, chickens were only served as a treat at Easter. But given that consumers have become used to very cheap chicken as part of their diet, both at home and in fast-food restaurants, and that in the UK alone we eat more than thirty-four million eggs every day – almost 200 for every man, woman and child in the country every year – that is unlikely to happen, at least in the short-term. The only ray of hope for the world's chickens is the recent breakthroughs in the development of synthetic 'meat'. Ironically, however, this could ultimately lead to the disappearance of the domestic chicken across much of the globe.

Another irony is that in the native range of the red junglefowl, across much of India and south-east Asia, the species is now in decline. Partly this is down to habitat loss, but also because free-range chickens, kept in and around villages, tend to wander off and breed with their wild cousins, producing hybrid offspring that dilute the wild population.

Four Colly Birds

BLACKBIRDS

When we hear 'The Twelve Days of Christmas' being sung, the usual refrain for the fourth line is 'four calling birds', which of course could refer to virtually any species.

But the original version has the line 'four *colly* birds'. In a way, it's not surprising that we rarely sing this, as it does not appear to make sense. 'Colly' is an archaic term, mainly used in the West Country, for the colour black. It derives from the word 'coaly', meaning 'coal-coloured', and is sometimes spelt 'collie', as in the black (and white) dog of the same name. So 'colly bird' simply means the blackbird.

The blackbird is one of the most common and familiar of all British birds, as the pioneering conservationist W. H. Hudson noted in 1895:

Among the feathered inhabitants of these islands there is scarcely a more familiar figure than that of the blackbird . . . His music is much to us, his beautiful mellow voice being unique in character . . . But, more than his voice, his love of gardens . . . is his blackness.

Indeed, of all our common garden birds, only the robin, house sparrow and perhaps the blue tit are as well-known, and only the robin better loved.

We take the blackbird's popularity for granted. Yet perhaps we shouldn't, for virtually every other 'black bird' – from rooks to ravens and crows to cormorants – is despised and denigrated, belittled and vilified, simply, one suspects, for being black, the colour often associated with the devil. In cultures and societies around the world, black has for centuries often symbolised all that is mysterious, dark or evil in human nature. As well as the obvious juxtaposition of darkness (black) with light (white), it has been appropriated to represent ignorance versus truth, death versus life, evil versus good and, in the murky world of racial politics, the repellent notion that the colour of a person's skin somehow makes them less of a human being than another individual.

True, black can also be positive: it is the most elegant colour in fashion (the 'little black dress'), while as the colour of mourning, it symbolises a serious and crucial phase in our lives. But overall its associations are usually negative, so its use in the name of a bird that has always been so popular is rather puzzling.

Perhaps as a result, there are several myths that seek to explain away the blackbird's colour, all of which suggest that it was originally pure white. One tale from Italy is linked to the *giorni della merla* or 'blackbird days' which occur each year on the last two days of January and the first day of February.

The story goes that one year it was so cold that the bird had to hide in a chimney and, when it finally emerged, the soot had turned its plumage black. In another (this time French) folk-tale, the blackbird was tempted by the evil magpie (another bird with plenty of black in its plumage) to enter the underworld to search for gold; when he did so, a demon chased him away, but by then he had turned black because of the fire and smoke.

The blackbird was not, however, always called by its current name. Until the fourteenth century, and often later, it would have been known as the 'ouzel' or 'ousel', a name that derives from Old English, and relates to the modern German name *Amsel*. Ouzel still lives on in the name of the blackbird's montane cousin, the ring ouzel, and in a now more or less obsolete folk-name for the dipper, 'water ouzel'. It also appears in Shakespeare's comedy *A Midsummer Night's Dream*, as 'The woosell cocke, so blacke of hew, with orange-tawny bill' – a clear reference to the male blackbird.

There are several reasons why blackbirds inspire affection rather than distrust, as crows do, for instance. The male bird's 'orange-tawny' (or as we might say, yellow) bill, along with the yellow rings around his eyes, give him an open, friendly appearance. Incidentally, the next line in our carol, 'five gold rings', has also been linked to the blackbird, being mistakenly supposed to represent the yellow ring around the male's eye.

The blackbird's habits, too, are mainly benevolent: they spend most of their time hopping around on our lawns or in the leaf-litter on the forest floor, searching for earthworms and other invertebrate prey. When we watch a male blackbird feeding, he seems to glance at us from time to time: in fact, he is tilting his head to one side to listen for the tiny movements of worms just beneath the surface of the ground.

And, like so many other species that originally evolved to live in woodland, the blackbird has readily adapted to our gardens. Here, it doesn't just survive, but thrives, thanks to a combination of ready-made places to roost and nest, and plenty of food on tap.

But if there is one thing about the blackbird that really propels the species up the popularity charts, it is its song. In spring, blackbirds start singing very early in the morning: the dawn chorus in a garden, park or ancient woodland usually kicks off with either the robin or the blackbird, often well before daybreak. Countless people have waxed lyrical about the beauty, melody and tone of the blackbird's song. In 1908, the popular nature writer William Percival Westell penned this paean to the bird:

> What more mellifluous songster could grace the opening of a work devoted to British bird life? The Blackbird is a favourite everywhere, and for good reasons. He is one of the kings of song, one of the chief choristers in Nature's great orchestra.

The nineteenth-century poet John Clare agreed:

> Hark at the melody howe rich and loud
> Like daylight breaking through the morning cloud
> How luscious through that sea of green it floats
> Knowest thou of music breathed from sweeter notes
> Than that wild minstrel of the summer shower
> Breathes at this moment from that hazel bower . . .

In his 1945 monograph *The Blackbird*, A. F. C. Hillstead was marginally more measured in his praise:

> [The Blackbird] possesses a really wonderful voice, and I have no
> hesitation in saying that it was the song which first roused my
> interest in the bird . . . The notes are rich in tone, possessing the
> purity of a wood-instrument . . . The delivery is lazy, and, on a hot
> day, gives the impression of sleepy contentment.

But not everyone has been quite so enthusiastic about the qualities of the blackbird's song; indeed, the Victorian ornithologist William Yarrell was rather dismissive:

> The song of the Blackbird is more remarkable for power and
> quality of tone than for compass or variety. It is usually much too
> loud . . . and the same notes are too frequently repeated.

At the risk of alienating many of my readers, I'm on Yarrell's side. For me, the blackbird's song is pedantic, slow and tedious: a predictable series of rather dull, monotonous phrases, delivered with little or no enthusiasm. I far prefer the song thrush, whose perky song, composed of a range of repeated notes and phrases, sounds as if it is engaging you in (an admittedly rather one-sided) conversation.

And sometimes the blackbird's song doesn't quite live up to people's high expectations. A decade or so ago, a contributor to the RSPB's Internet Forum asked her fellow-members for help:

I was wondering if anyone could shed any light on why our resident blackbird 'sings' the way it does.

Blackbirds usually have a varied and melodic song, which is beautiful and relaxing to listen to. Our resident blackbird is sadly incapable of this and is only able to shout out pretty much one note in a fast-paced '*chirrup chirrup*' fashion. The call is virtually incessant from 2 a.m. to 11 p.m. every day. Occasionally it will fly across the gardens shouting out the panic-stricken cry blackbirds sing . . . having seemingly been disturbed by something. Other than that, it incessantly chirrups in one note, pausing for nothing. We have never seen or heard it sing the usual blackbird song.

I appreciate I can probably do little to stop it doing this and driving me mad, but I was wondering why it is doing this all day, every day for weeks and weeks. Has anyone else had a seeming unlyrical blackbird or know why my resident blackbird is melodically challenged?

One suggestion was that this might be a young and inexperienced male blackbird, trying out its song. We never did find out if it managed to improve.

But, given that Thomas Bewick noted that 'the young birds are easily tamed, and may be taught to whistle a variety of tunes,' it seems odd that even a young bird would be quite so unmelodic.

The blackbird's familiarity is at least partly explained by its ubiquity. When I was growing up, in the 1960s, it was considered, along with the chaffinch, to be the most numerous bird in Britain. Today, both have slipped down the league table behind the wren and the robin: the chaffinch is now third and the blackbird fourth, with about 4.9 million breeding pairs. But by being present in 96 per cent of all the 3,862 10-kilometre squares in Britain and Ireland, in both summer and winter, it is as ubiquitous as any species apart from the wren. If we bear in mind that its cousin the ring ouzel effectively replaces the blackbird in many upland areas, at least one of this 'species-pair' can be found in virtually every square. And, unlike many songbirds, the blackbird is doing rather well: in the past thirty years or so, numbers have risen by about a quarter.

The reason the blackbird has bucked the trend, at least compared with its relatives the song and mistle thrushes, both of which have declined over the same period, is its ability to live in gardens. At first sight, a small suburban garden – or even a large, rural one – might appear to be a less promising place to set up home than an ancient woodland. But appearances can be deceptive: studies have shown that blackbirds breed at higher densities in villages, towns and cities – especially on suburban housing estates – reaching up to seven pairs a hectare (or about

Black Birds

eight to eleven pairs in an area the size of a standard football pitch). That's roughly two or three times as many pairs in a given area as you would find in a traditional woodland.

There may be several reasons for this surprising statistic. The main one is food: like other garden birds, blackbirds take full advantage of the free and easily available food we provide, day after day, on our bird tables. That means that they can stay put all year round, whereas rural blackbirds are more likely to have to travel away from their breeding areas in winter, some migrating a fair distance.

This also means that city birds can begin breeding earlier, and finish later, than their country cousins: blackbirds usually have two or three broods a year, but can have as many as five. The survival of those chicks again depends on food. They may also benefit from the 'urban heat-island' effect, in which cities are several degrees warmer than the surrounding countryside, especially in winter, because of the heat generated from traffic and buildings. All these are good reasons for any small bird to head into the city.

But it's not all easy for urban blackbirds: there are far more cats in most towns and cities than there are in the countryside and, as low-flying birds, they are often killed by traffic as they cross over from one side of a leafy avenue to the other. And although we may welcome long hot summers, when they do occur, and lawns dry out and harden, blackbirds in gardens struggle to get to their favourite food of earthworms.

In a typical year, blackbirds will build a neat, cup-shaped nest out of grass, lined with mud, during March; and lay their first clutch of three or four eggs during the first half of April. In very mild winters, they will start to nest far earlier – occasionally even before the New Year – though such abnormally early clutches rarely, if ever, survive through to fledging.

This habit may have given rise to the folk-rhyme 'When the blackbird sings before Christmas, she will cry before Candlemas,' meaning that if a pair starts to breed before 25 December, it will have failed by 2 February. Yet if mild winters eventually become the norm, as a result of climate change, perhaps December and January broods of blackbirds will become commonplace.

I can still remember that, when I was a child, a pair of blackbirds used to nest each year in the clematis outside our kitchen window. I would watch the female sneaking in and out, and occasionally take a peek at the clutch of greenish-blue eggs, speckled with reddish-brown, as if with a child's paintbrush. By then, the boyhood pastime of egg-collecting had virtually died out, and was actually against the law; yet a residual kleptomaniac urge remained.

I must admit that I did take a blackbird's egg (not from our garden nest, as that would have seemed rude), and hid it in the airing cupboard in my grandmother's bedroom for several weeks, in the hope that it might hatch. By the time I had lost patience, and decided to 'blow' the egg to add it to my non-existent collection, it had 'addled'. As I blew, it cracked; then split open, to reveal a long-dead chick. I never took another bird's egg again.

If a blackbird's clutch does survive the twin threats of cats and small boys, the eggs will hatch just a couple of weeks after they were laid. Like other songbirds, the chicks are born naked and blind, though their survival instinct impels them to respond with wide-open bills, pointed straight up in the air, every time a parent returns with a morsel of food. They grow very fast indeed: by the time they are just over two weeks old they have shed their down and grown their first feathers, and are ready to leave the nest.

But the odds are roughly fifty-fifty that they will survive their first year. Even if they do, they are unlikely to live much beyond their third birthday – though the oldest ringed bird managed to reach the advanced age of fourteen years, nine months and twenty-five days.

Blackbirds may not be celebrated by poets quite as much as the skylark or nightingale – or even the robin and song thrush – but they do nevertheless appear in some of our finest poetical works. Of these, perhaps the best-known is the short yet lyrically powerful poem 'Adlestrop', written by Edward Thomas.

Thomas published the poem in 1916, halfway through the First World War, in which he served in the British Army. But it was based on a railway journey he had taken two years earlier, on 24 June 1914, less than six weeks before the war's outbreak. As the train trundled slowly towards its eventual destination, it stopped for a few moments at the halt just outside the Gloucestershire village of Adlestrop, where the poet's attention was caught by a snatch of birdsong:

> And for that minute a blackbird sang
> Close by, and round him, mistier,
> Farther and farther, all the birds
> Of Oxfordshire and Gloucestershire.

The peacefulness of the verse is in direct contrast to the horrors that were soon to follow; horrors that ultimately claimed the life of the poet himself, who was killed at the Battle of Arras, in northern France, on 9 April 1917.

A more light-hearted – though nevertheless rather puzzling – representation of the blackbird appears in the nursery rhyme 'Sing a Song of Sixpence':

> Sing a song of sixpence,
> A pocket full of rye.
> Four and twenty blackbirds,
> Baked in a pie.
>
> When the pie was opened
> The birds began to sing;
> Wasn't that a dainty dish,
> To set before the king.

Dating back to the eighteenth century (though it may of course be far older than that), 'Sing a Song of Sixpence' – and in particular the reference to two dozen blackbirds 'baked in a pie' – is thought to refer to a rather odd culinary custom, popular around the time of the Renaissance, during the sixteenth century. This involved putting a second, separately-cooked layer of pastry over the baked surface of a pie, beneath which live – though presumably rather distressed – birds would be hidden. When the pie was cut, they would then fly out, to the surprise, and apparent delight, of the guests.

This was just one of a range of different food-based entertainments known as an 'entremets' (from the Old French meaning 'between courses'), in which the actual food served to the diners appears to have been less important than its entertainment value. Given the habit of many birds of defecating when under stress, one can only presume that in those days, diners had stronger stomachs than we do.

Interestingly, there have been numerous attempts to find a hidden meaning in the rhyme, including the idea that the blackbirds might represent the devil (again, because they are black), the number of hours in a day, or a reference to the Bible. But no evidence has ever been found to support any of these theories, and the traditional culinary explanation seems far more likely.

Perhaps the best-known evocation of the blackbird – or more specifically, its song – comes not from a conventional poet, nor an anonymous author of a nursery rhyme, but one of our greatest songwriters and musicians: Paul McCartney of the Beatles. He wrote the song 'Blackbird' in 1968, and it later appeared on *The Beatles* (more usually known as 'The White Album'). It is one of the few popular music recordings that actually reproduces birdsong as part of the track, as an accompaniment to the singer and his acoustic guitar.

Over the years, the song has been subject to countless interpretations: many plausible, others rather fanciful, and some – including those given by McCartney himself – frankly contradictory. It may be a message of support to the nascent Black Power movement; or it may contain a more philosophical message about the transcendent nature of the human soul. Or it may, of course, simply be about a blackbird.

But was the bird McCartney was listening to really *Turdus merula*, the common or Eurasian blackbird – or could it perhaps have been a completely different species? Various accounts of the song's origin suggest it was written either in India, where the Beatles were visiting the Maharishi Mahesh Yogi, or in Scotland.

If the former, it is unlikely to have been inspired by the song of a blackbird, as the species is not found in India. If the latter, it is more likely to have been a mistle thrush, which has a similar tone to a blackbird's song; or a robin, one of the few species that habitually sings, like the bird in the song, 'in the dead of night'.

Writing a century and a half earlier, John Clare was well aware that the song of the blackbird could easily be confused with that of other species: 'The blackbird has often been said to sing in winter . . . but very rarely and the song of the Mavis [song] thrush is often mistaken for that of the blackbird.'

Five Gold Rings

YELLOWHAMMERS

Admit it: has it never occurred to you that there is something rather odd about the fifth line of 'The Twelve Days of Christmas'? Why would the generous donor suddenly switch to jewellery, when all the other gifts are not only animated but, as I believe, related to birds?

I too, was puzzled by this strange anomaly until, when researching my book on the origins of bird names, *Mrs Moreau's Warbler*, I came across a now long-forgotten folk-name for the yellowhammer: 'yoldring'.

Like so many folk-names, this dated from a time when the predominant form of discourse would have been the spoken rather than the written word. So 'yoldring' would have been spelt in several different ways, including 'youldring', 'yeldrin', 'yaldrin', 'yorling', 'yourling' and 'yowlring'. These date back at least as early as the late seventeenth century, though were probably in use far earlier. The word 'yellow' was often added as a prefix, as in this first recorded written usage in 1699, by the pioneering Scottish scientist Robert Sibbald: 'The Common Linet, the Bunting, the Goldfinch, the Thistle Cock, the Yellow Yeldring.'

In 1810, the poet Robert Tannahill, born and bred in Paisley, also referred to the folk-name in this evocative verse:

> Beneath the golden gloaming sky,
> The mavis [thrush] mends her lay,
> The redbreast [robin] pours his sweetest strains,
> To charm the ling'ring day,
> While weary yeldrins seem to wail
> Their little nestlings torn,
> The merry wren, frae den to den,
> Gaes jinking through the thorn.

And a decade later, in his 1820 novel *Abbot*, Sir Walter Scott used the name in a striking simile about an imbalance of power: 'You heed me no more than a goss-hawk minds a yellow yoldring.'

Even Robert Burns got in on the act, with his highly suggestive poem (often sung) 'The Yellow, Yellow Yorlin', which ends with the narrator's sexual conquest of his 'pretty maid':

> But I teuk her by the waist, an laid her doun in haste,
> For a' her squakin an squalin;
> The lassie suin grew tame, an bade me come again
> For to play wi her yellow yellow yorlin.

What all these references to the name 'yoldring' and its variants have in common is that they come from Scottish writers. That's because the name was unknown in southern Britain, but commonplace in northern England, Ireland and Scotland.

It seems very likely to me that whoever translated this carol from French to English knew of the folk-name for the bird, which neatly fits the metre of the verse. However, when faced with the unfamiliar term 'yoldrings', listeners to the carol naturally assumed it meant 'gold rings': the line we have sung ever since!

This is not at all unusual. Time and again, when people are faced with an unfamiliar word or phrase, they tend to turn it into something that – to them at least – does make sense, as in the previous line in the carol, in which 'colly birds' often becomes '*calling* birds'. I've lost count of the times I've heard carol singers recite the line from 'We Wish You a Merry Christmas' as 'Good tidings we bring, to you and your *king*,' when the correct word is of course 'kin', meaning family. There are two reasons for this particular change: not only does 'king' rhyme with 'bring', but the word 'kin' is rapidly falling out of use.

The yellowhammer is the commonest and most widespread member of its family in Europe, and can be found across much of the vast Eurasian landmass, from Ireland and northern Portugal in the west, to the Caucasus and central Siberia in the east, where it overlaps (and often hybridises) with its sister species, the pine bunting. It is very adaptable, often nesting at high as well as low elevations, and breeding beyond the Arctic Circle in northern Scandinavia where, each autumn, the population heads south for the winter.

In Britain, the yellowhammer can still be found across much of the lowland countryside, though it is now absent from many upland areas, including those of Wales and Scotland. Surveys also show that, as a breeding bird, it is far more widespread in the east of Britain than the west.

Females are, especially when seen at a distance, basically brown in appearance. But a closer view allows us to see the yellowish shades on the cheeks, throat, breast and belly, and the chestnut shading, streaked with dark brown, on the back. Their subdued plumage is because they incubate the eggs alone, with no help from the male, and so need to be better camouflaged than he is.

But the male has no such need to hide away his charms. As a result, he is a truly beautiful creature, especially during the spring and summer, when he adopts his full breeding plumage. Like his mate, he has chestnut and dark-brown streaks across his back and wings, but his head, face, neck, throat, breast and belly are a bright custard-yellow, with fine brown streaking on

his underparts, and darker stripes behind the eye and across the crown. During the autumn and winter, the male loses some of his bright yellow tones, and becomes rather duller. Both male and female yellowhammers also sport a plain, bright, chestnut-coloured rump, most often seen as they fly away from you along the hedgerow.

Getting back to names, the official name for *Emberiza citrinella* – the 'yellowhammer' – has long caused confusion, again because the original meaning has become obscured, and we have replaced a puzzling, unfamiliar word with a familiar one. *Ammer* is the German word for bunting, as in the German name for the species, *Goldammer*.

The word 'ammer' came over with the original Anglo-Saxon invaders, and was used in the species' name. But after 1066, when Norman French began to replace the Old English terms, it no longer made sense, so 'ammer' turned into 'hammer', by exactly the same process of misunderstanding as 'yoldring' became 'gold rings'. So today, while all the other members of the family have the epithet 'bunting' – corn, reed, snow, cirl, Lapland and so on – the yellowhammer stubbornly retains its original name.

One widely used folk-name for the species is 'scribble lark' (or sometimes 'writing lark'), because of the pencil-like markings on its eggs. I recall once giving a talk on bird names in Somerset, and an elderly man in the audience telling of how, when he and his pals used to hunt for birds' eggs, they always knew when they had found a yellowhammer's clutch because of this distinctive scribbled pattern.

When talking about the yellowhammer, it doesn't usually take long for the conversation to turn to another famous aspect of the bird's character: its song. This is because of an aide-mémoire we use to help us remember which species is singing: 'A-little-bit-of-bread-and-no-cheeeese . . .'

One reason why so many people are aware of this useful phrase is that the bestselling children's author Enid Blyton referred to it several times: it appears in her 'Famous Five' story *Five Go Off in a Caravan,* as well as in *The Ship of Adventure.* She also wrote about the bird in her 1944 non-fiction work *Enid Blyton's Nature-Lover's Book*, which included a poem devoted to 'The Yellowhammer Bird'.

When I was a child, this was one of the very first bird songs I managed to learn; helped, no doubt, by that curious, yet memorable mnemonic. The sound is redolent of lazy days in the middle of summer for, as Gilbert White noted, yellowhammers, like other members of the bunting family, sing longer and later into the summer season than most other songbirds:

> I heard many birds of several species sing last year after midsummer; enough to prove that the summer solstice is not the period that puts a stop to the music of the woods. The yellowhammer no doubt persists with more steadiness than any other.

As to whether the mnemonic is actually accurate, that might be up for discussion. It certainly captures the overall rhythm of the song, but to my ears is a bit too varied for what is, essentially, a quick-fire series of double notes followed by a long, wheezy ending.

The conservationist W. H. Hudson, writing at the turn of the twentieth century, recalled that 'the Scottish peasants' (his words, not mine) had what he called 'some curious superstitions about the yellow yoldring, as they call it':

> To them its song sounds like the words 'Deil, deil, deil tak ye,' and the bird itself is supposed to be on very familiar terms with the evil being whose name it evokes so freely, and who supplies it on a May morning with a drop of his own blood with which to paint its curiously marked eggs.

In a rather grisly custom, according to the folklorist Lewis R. Loyd, Scottish children would 'hang by the neck every Yellowhammer they could get hold of', again presumably because of that supposed link with the Devil. An even more unpleasant game involved taking the yellowhammer's unfledged young (known as 'gorbals') from their nest, and hanging them by their necks from a crossbeam, using a thread, with a small stone to balance the suspended bird. The delinquent children would then strike the stone and launch the unfortunate bird into the air, in a game they called 'spangle-hewit', meaning 'elastic-head'.

For both Hudson and Loyd, the yellowhammer would have been as familiar as any other common bird of the countryside: nesting in the thick, broad hedgerows between the fields, and feeding in winter on the seeds left with the stubble, and in summer on the plentiful insects feeding on the wild flowers along the edge of every field.

A century earlier, Thomas Bewick could write that 'this bird is common in every lane and hedge, flitting before the traveller as he passes along, or uttering its simple and frequently repeated monotone,' while in the 1850s William MacGillivray, based in and around Aberdeen, also suggested that the bird was so common it was hardly worth considering: 'The Yellow Bunting, although neither inelegant in form, nor deficient in richness of colouring, is so common that it attracts little attention.'

It is a pity that MacGillivray was quite so dismissive of the yellowhammer, for, as he grudgingly points out, it is actually a very attractive little bird. The character of the yellowhammer was beautifully captured by the mid-twentieth-century Scottish poet Andrew Young:

> All up the grassy many-tracked sheep walk,
> Low sun on my right hand, hedge on my left,
> Blotted by a late leaf, else leaf bereft,
> I drove my golden flock.
>
> Yellow-hammers, gold-headed, russet-backed,
> They fled in jerky flight before my feet,
> Or pecked in the green ranks of winter wheat,
> While I my footsteps slacked.

It's hardly surprising that John Clare also wrote about the yellow-hammer; or more specifically, its nest, showing off his

When it comes to breeding, it seems rather odd that the yellow-hammer – a resident species, present on its farmland habitat all year round – should choose to nest so much later in the summer than other birds. The reason is that, although the female lays her first clutch of eggs in late April or May, she will have a second brood in June, and often a third in July or August – and the male will keep singing throughout that period.

The female builds the cup-shaped nest, woven out of leaves, stalks and grasses and lined with hair from livestock animals and finer grasses, often on or near the ground, and carefully hidden away from predators such as rats, mice and crows. She lays between three and five eggs, and when they hatch, between twelve and fourteen days after incubation begins, the male joins in with the work of finding food for the chicks.

Like other small songbirds, the yellowhammer's young are born naked, blind and helpless. But they grow rapidly, and the time spent tending the chicks is fairly short: just eleven to thirteen days, before the fledglings leave the safety of the nest.

After the final brood of young have safely fledged, both male and female become far less easy to see, as they take advantage of the long late summer days and plentiful availability of food to moult, the males becoming more and more yellow with each year's plumage change, which presumably makes them even more attractive to potential mates. Like other songbirds, however, yellowhammers do not live very long: typically, both adults and juveniles have just a fifty-fifty chance of surviving from one year to the next, and rarely live longer than the age of three;

though odd individuals have managed to survive for more than a decade.

If you ask any countryman or -woman aged sixty or over about the yellowhammer, they are likely to say that they know it well, even if, perhaps, they haven't actually seen one for a few years. That's because until recently it was one of the commonest birds of rural Britain, found in hedgerows throughout much of England, Wales, Scotland and Northern Ireland. But younger folk, even those born and bred in rural parts, may no longer be quite so familiar with this attractive little yellow bird.

Today, the yellowhammer is, like so many other farmland species – including the skylark, corn bunting, linnet, and two others featured in this book, the grey partridge and turtle dove – now in decline. Unlike the other species, however, its fall in numbers seems to have begun rather later: from the late 1980s onwards. We still have no idea why this should have been.

But when the decline did finally happen, it accelerated remarkably quickly. During the late 1990s, yellowhammer numbers were falling at the astonishing rate of 10 per cent a year – clearly unsustainable should this continue. In the forty years from 1970 to 2010, the total population of yellowhammers in Britain dropped by more than half.

Along with a fall in numbers came a contraction in the yellowhammer's distribution: in Ireland, on the extreme western edge of its range, over a third of the area where the bird had been present in the original 1968-72 breeding *Atlas* had by 1988-91 been abandoned. Even in Britain, it disappeared from one-fifth of its previous range in less than twenty years.

As with so many other species that depend on our farmed countryside, we can pinpoint the reasons for the yellowhammer's decline. In spring and summer, the parent birds need to find plenty of insects and other invertebrates for their hungry brood of young. Typically, these include spiders, flies, caterpillars, beetles, earthworms and even snails, which are fed to the chicks during their first two or three days of life. From then on, the parents gradually switch to a diet based on seeds and grains, including those of wheat, oats, docks and various grasses, which they find by foraging on the ground.

On traditional mixed farms, or amongst less intensive cereal crops with plenty of nectar-rich wild flowers, finding this variety of insects and seeds is not a problem; but on highly intensive arable land sown with crops, or where grass is grown for silage, the birds often struggle to find food.

Even if a pair of yellowhammers does manage to fledge one or more broods of young, they then need to find enough food to survive during the following autumn and winter. Again, changes in the way we farm have affected them: the widespread planting of winter wheat means there are no longer fields covered with stubble, where the birds can join mixed flocks of sparrows, finches and other buntings to feed on seeds, on which they depend for much of the year.

As with all farmland creatures, from birds to butterflies to bumblebees, the only way to reverse the yellowhammer's decline would be to farm in a more wildlife-friendly way: creating a mosaic of habitats during all four seasons of the year so that the birds can find enough food. At the moment, that does not seem very likely, and the yellowhammer will no doubt remain on the Red List of Birds of Conservation Concern for some time yet.

Given that many of the problems faced by the yellowhammer and other farmland species come from the much-hated Common Agricultural Policy, it is ironic that the contingency plan put in place by the British government to cope with a no-deal Brexit, from late 2018 onwards, was dubbed 'Operation Yellowhammer'. As Bill Oddie tweeted indignantly, 'Outrage! Keep our birds out of this mayhem please. Especially ones that are decreasing, due largely to British farming regime.'

There is one place, however, where yellowhammers are still thriving: 12,000 miles away on the other side of the globe, in New Zealand. Unfortunately, it is for all the wrong reasons. During the Victorian era, organisations known as 'Acclimatisation Societies' sprang up across the British Empire and other parts of the world. Their stated aim was to 'improve and enrich' the fauna and flora of our distant colonies by bringing over and releasing familiar British species.

This had, so its proponents believed, two major benefits: first, the supposedly impoverished local wildlife would become more diverse and interesting; and secondly, expatriate settlers would have something familiar to remind them of home. Songbirds were especially welcome, and in New Zealand these included the greenfinch, goldfinch, lesser redpoll, starling, house sparrow, dunnock and the yellowhammer's scarcer cousin, the cirl bunting.

Thus it was that during the 1860s and 1870s, only a few years after the British Acclimatisation Society had been founded, 600 yellowhammers of the British and Irish subspecies were brought over to New Zealand and released. Within a few years they had spread across the two main landmasses, North and South Island, ultimately reaching many offshore islands.

Although the arrival of the yellowhammer and other songbirds was not as disastrous for New Zealand as the introduction of rabbits and foxes, it still had a hugely negative affect on the delicate native ecosystem of this remote archipelago, as well as its farming. By the start of the twentieth century, yellowhammers were considered a serious agricultural pest, because of their consumption of newly-sown seeds; a bounty was even put on their heads to encourage people to shoot and trap them.

By then, the realisation that acclimatisation societies had been little short of a disaster was finally taking root: the last shipment of birds, in 1880, was never released into the wild. But it was too late: the yellowhammers were far too numerous and widespread to be eradicated. Even today, they breed at much higher densities there than do their cousins back home.

In 2017, a fascinating story about these yellowhammers appeared in the press. Czech scientists had compared recordings made of singing males in New Zealand and Britain with each other, and discovered something surprising. Because the New Zealand birds had nearly twice as many different song-types, or dialects, as their counterparts back home, the scientists concluded that some were singing songs that would not have been heard in Britain for over 150 years, creating what has been described as a 'living archive'. The researchers compared this with the way that now-obsolete English words and phrases often survive in far-flung colonies, long after they have disappeared in Britain.

It's ironic that, as our own, native population of yellowhammers continues to decline, the very sound that once made the bird such a familiar part of rural Britain is under threat; and that, if we want to hear the yellowhammer's celebrated song in all its glory, we must now travel to the other side of the world.

Six Geese A-Laying

GEESE

There are few natural spectacles more impressive than a flock of wild geese passing overhead at dawn or dusk. From Norfolk in the south to Islay in the north, and many places in between, it is possible to witness vast flocks of geese leaving their night-time roost as dawn breaks on a chilly winter's day, and then flying in that characteristic V-formation, as they head out into the surrounding fields to feed. Come back an hour or so before dusk, and they can be seen again, as they return to the safety of their roost.

At both morning and evening, this stirring sight of these birds against the sky is accompanied by their haunting, honking calls – the way the birds communicate with one another, and also announce their presence to the human, earthbound world below.

Geese in numbers have a magical quality about them, and yet as individual birds they can sometimes seem awkward and clumsy. That's especially true when they waddle along on the ground, so different from that graceful presence in the air. It is almost as if they need to be appreciated *en masse*, when they combine to take on a very different way of being; based on the collective, rather than the individual.

Thomas Bewick, writing at the turn of the nineteenth century, was one of the first observers to note the almost mathematical quality of wild goose flocks:

> This elevated and marshalled flight of the Wild Geese seems dictated by geometrical instinct: shaped like a wedge, they cut through the air with less individual exertion; and it is conjectured, that the change [in formation] . . . is occasioned by the leader . . . quitting his post at the point of the angle through fatigue, dropping into the rear, and leaving his place to be occupied by another.

Bewick was quite correct to infer that the V-shaped flying formations of geese had evolved to allow them to save energy, by making the flock as a whole more aerodynamic. This is especially important on long, migratory journeys, when the danger of tiring out and plummeting exhausted into the sea below is very real.

Yet for Bewick, wild geese would have been far less familiar than the tame, domesticated variety. In the second volume of his pioneering *History of British Birds*, devoted to 'Water Birds', he included this detailed and revealing account of the way geese used to be kept:

> The Gozzard (Goose-herd) takes them out onto the marshes in spring and summer – especially in the fens of Lincolnshire, where it is said to be no uncommon thing for a single person to keep a thousand old Geese, each of which, on an average, will bring up seven young ones.

Bewick also went on to outline the 'unfeeling, greedy business' of plucking the geese for their quills and feathers, which took place up to five times a year, starting on Lady Day, 25 March, and ending on Michaelmas Day, six months later, on 29 September. He also wrote of how the fattened birds, now ready for eating, were taken to market:

> To the country market town they are carried in bags and panniers; to the great centre of trade they are sent in droves of many thousands. To a stranger it is a most curious spectacle to view these hissing, cackling, gabbling, but peaceful armies . . . waddling on (like other armies) to certain destruction.

Although a city-dweller himself – he lived in Newcastle upon Tyne – Bewick reserved wry contempt for some of his fellow citizens, who were blissfully unaware of the realities of nature: 'A certain town lady wondered how a Goose could suckle nine Goslings.'

Domestication – the capturing, keeping and breeding of wild animals for use by humans – is perhaps the oldest example of our longstanding dominion over the natural world. The dog is thought to be the first wild animal to have been domesticated, from a now extinct population of grey wolves back in the Pleistocene era, roughly 15,000 years ago. Goats, pigs, sheep and cattle soon followed, but it was not until around 7,400 years ago that the first species of bird – the red junglefowl of the Indian subcontinent – was domesticated, as what would eventually become the chicken (see Chapter 3).

Wild ducks – specifically the mallard – were domesticated around 6,000 years ago, while the rock dove started to become the domestic pigeon a millennium later. About the same time – roughly 3000 BC, or 5,000 years before the present – the greylag goose (in Egypt) and the swan goose (in China), were also domesticated. Sometime before then the name 'goose', or something like it, had already been coined in the ur-language now known as 'Proto-Indo-European', making it probably the oldest bird name still in existence.

Domestic – or, as they are often called, 'farmyard' – geese turned out to be even more useful than their original captors might have imagined. They are voracious feeders, and their large size means that a well-fattened goose (weighing up to 10 kg, compared to just four kg in the wild) can provide plenty of food for a whole family. Through selective breeding, they have been encouraged to lay large, nutritious eggs: up to 300 each year, compared with just five to twelve eggs a year for their wild counterparts. As a result of these changes, domestic geese are not only larger and heavier than their wild cousins, but also a distinctively different shape: pot-bellied, with a broader rear end and more upright posture. This is especially true of the geese that are cruelly force-fed to produce the epicurean delicacy foie gras.

Geese also have a fine set of feathers: soft, downy ones suitable for a range of uses including stuffing pillows and cushions, and the larger stronger wing-feathers, which later on (probably around the second century BC) were turned into quill pens, and used to write the famous Dead Sea Scrolls.

What their new owners might not have expected is that domestic geese have another surprisingly useful quality: as the avian equivalent of guard dogs. As Thomas Bewick noted, 'The Goose has for many ages been celebrated on account of its vigilance . . . It is on account of this property that they are esteemed . . . as the most vigilant of sentinels.' The best-known story of 'guard-geese' comes from Ancient Rome. Two thousand four hundred years ago, the city was being sacked by the invading Gauls, and the empire was under threat as never before. At first, the Gauls were successful, conquering the whole of the city apart from one site, the Capitoline Hill, which the Romans were still desperately managing to defend.

Then one night, the Gauls planned a surprise raid on this final citadel. But just as they were approaching their target, they disturbed a flock of geese, which started honking frantically. The noise awoke the Roman guards, who managed to repel the invaders. Eventually they won back control, and the Roman Empire continued to thrive and expand – ultimately invading Britain.

It is interesting, though perhaps fruitless, to wonder how the course of history might have changed had those vigilant geese not sounded the alarm. But this raises another question: why, given that the Romans were under siege and presumably suffering from acute food shortages, had these birds not already been killed and eaten? The answer is that these were sacred creatures, living in the temple of Juno, the goddess of fertility (specifically of marriage, pregnancy and childbirth). So eating them – even under such difficult circumstances – would have been taboo.

Geese are still often used as guards – they are cheaper and

easier to keep than dogs – but, as with their canine counterparts, their enthusiasm in repelling intruders can sometimes cause problems. In 2001, a goose in Illinois attacked a delivery worker, who successfully sued the offending company for $17,000. Yet even this settlement was dwarfed by a lawsuit in Buffalo, New York, when a woman attacked by a goose while on a neighbour's property won a whopping $2.4 million in damages. And in an echo of the urban myth that 'a swan can break a man's arm,' Canada geese have been known to knock people down in parks, resulting in fractures of their arms or legs.

Mention of Canada geese brings me back to the original, wild version of the bird. Geese are members of the family Anatidae, which comprises more than 160 different species of ducks, geese and swans. Roughly thirty members of this family have 'goose' in their name, but only seventeen of these are 'true geese', of the genera *Anser* (the larger 'grey geese'), *Chen* (the white 'snow geese') and *Branta* (the mostly smaller 'black geese').

The true geese are all northern hemisphere species, whose ranges go from Hawaii in the south and west, to Japan in the east and way beyond the Arctic Circle in the north. Of those seventeen species, twelve have been seen in the wild in Britain, with eight being regular visitors, though only three species – the wild and feral greylag goose, the introduced Canada goose, and a small feral population of barnacle geese – actually breed.

Because they are non-native, and perhaps because they originally hail from North America, we have an ambivalent attitude towards Canada geese. They have now been here a very long time – the first birds were brought across the Atlantic and kept in

London's St James's Park in the late seventeenth century – yet we have never really taken them to our hearts.

At one point, visitors to London parks, fed up with the mess the flocks of Canada geese create with their sloppy green droppings, and their tendency to be aggressive towards passers-by and small children, suggested a cull; but, after a protest led by the comedy writer and animal welfare supporter Carla Lane, the plans were quietly dropped. In their native North America, Canada geese are regarded with far greater affection and respect: as in the 1996 children's movie *Fly Away Home*, starring Jeff Daniels and Anna Paquin. Based on a true story, this shows how a man and his young daughter manage to train injured geese to learn to migrate again.

In Britain, geese are primarily winter visitors, which travel here each autumn from breeding grounds to the north, west and east, to take advantage of our very mild winter climate (at least for our relatively northerly latitude, thanks to the warming influence of the Gulf Stream).

Britain is internationally important for a number of different species, including the pink-footed goose, of which 80 per cent of the entire world population spends the winter here. So while the total breeding population of geese in Britain is a little over 100,000 pairs (the majority of these being Canada geese), this is dwarfed by the number of wintering geese: an estimated total of close to one million birds.

A million geese need an awful lot of food, and at times this has caused major problems between farmers and landowners on the one hand, and birders and conservationists on the other. The farmers resent the birds eating their crops – anything from potatoes and sugar beet to cereal crops such as winter wheat – and also the damage so many geese can do to the soil, by the constant trampling of their feet, and their acidic droppings. The conservationists point to the fact that Britain and Ireland are amongst the most important places in the world for these migratory birds, so they deserve our protection.

In the late twentieth century, matters came to a head on the Scottish island of Islay. Better known for its fine malt whisky than its birds, the island is nevertheless the winter home of internationally important numbers of two key species: the barnacle goose, and the Greenland subspecies of the white-fronted goose.

The 'barnies', as they are affectionately known, travel here from their breeding grounds in eastern Greenland. Close to two-thirds of the entire British and Irish wintering population – and more than half the world population – is found on Islay. For the Greenland white-fronts, the island is even more crucial: the entire world population of this distinctive, orange-billed race is just over 20,000 birds. The vast majority of these overwinter in Britain and Ireland, with Islay hosting more than a quarter.

So when, back in the 1980s, local farmers began taking the law into their own hands and shooting the geese, an urgent solution needed to be found. Careful work by the RSPB, and the granting of over £1 million a year in compensation to affected farmers, did appear to have solved the problem; indeed, the project was hailed as a textbook example of how to move 'from conflict to co-existence'.

But in recent years, following a huge rise in numbers of barnacle geese on Islay, Scottish Natural Heritage has begun a new cull of the birds, killing more than 3,000 every winter. This is despite evidence suggesting that many geese are wounded rather than killed, and that in any case the cull does not make any significant difference. This is a classic issue in which conservation and farming clash, with the birds as the casualties of human conflict.

Given the importance of geese in our lives, and especially their central place in our folklore and culture, this is a great pity. For generations, people have gazed up into the sky each autumn, prompted by honking sounds in the distance, and welcomed the returning flocks of geese. As with so many seasonal phenomena, our ancestors – and peoples from right across the northern hemisphere – regarded the timing of the birds' arrival as a sign that the coming winter would either be mild and wet, or cold and icy.

Martinmas (the feast day of St. Martin), which falls on 11 November, was, like many other saints' days, a key date in nature's calendar. If it coincided with a spell of unseasonably warm weather, it would be called 'goose summer'. The word 'gossamer', the fine webs spun by tiny spiders, derives from this phrase, as this phenomenon was linked to the arrival of migrating geese. But if the weather was unusually cold, a mild winter was predicted, as in the saying: 'If the geese at Martin's day stand on ice, they will walk in mud at Christmas.'

Other weather lore suggests that if geese fly high, it will be cold; if they fly low, mild weather should be expected. Likewise, if they fly to the sea, the weather will be good; if they head into the hills, then it will rain, as in this Morayshire rhyme:

> Wild geese, wild geese, ganging to the sea,
> Good weather it will be:
> Wild geese, wild geese, ganging to the hill,
> The weather it will spill.

However, as with so much weather-related folklore, these beliefs have absolutely no basis in fact. Like other wild creatures, birds are simply not able to predict the weather for the season to come.

What we do know is that geese, just like other migrant and overwintering birds, are able to react to sudden and imminent changes in the weather. So when large flocks of geese unexpect-edly arrive in Britain during the middle of winter, especially in the east of the country, it is usually an indication of freezing weather on the near-continent.

Various words and phrases related to geese – including 'gan-der', for the male, and 'goose', which usually refers to the female – have also entered our everyday language. If a person's 'goose is cooked', they are in big trouble, to 'take a gander' means to look more closely, while 'a wild goose chase' is a proverbial waste of time and effort. Less frequently used phrases, at least nowadays, include 'All his geese are swans', which suggests that the person mentioned tends to exaggerate; and 'What's sauce for the goose is sauce for the gander', meaning that what is acceptable to one person should also be acceptable to another. And despite the goose's reputation as a guard, they are proverbially regarded as rather stupid: hence the mild Victorian insult, 'silly goose'.

The *Oxford English Dictionary* gives no fewer than 75 examples of compound words formed from 'goose', of which my favour-ite is 'goose-turd green', popular around the time of Shake-speare, which refers to a dingy, greenish-yellow shade, the colour of goose droppings.

Geese also feature widely in other aspects of our folklore and mythology. One theory about the rather odd name of the barnacle goose is that it was called after its resemblance to that strange crustacean, the goose barnacle. These are filter-feed-ers, that attach themselves to the surfaces of rocks and various items of flotsam and jetsam in intertidal areas, especially piec-es of driftwood. When covered with water, the shells open and expose what looks uncannily like a goose's neck. At some point in ancient times, the similarity between the barnacles and the neck of the goose was noticed and, as the story has it, the bird was named after the crustacean. The pioneering sixteenth century ornithologist William Turner, who analysed the (often inaccurate) ornithological writings of the classical scholars Aristotle and Pliny, fell hook, line and sinker for this bizarre belief:

> No one has seen the Bernicle's nest or egg . . . since Bernicles without a parent's aid are said to have spontaneous generation in this way: when after a certain time the firwood masts or planks or yard-arms of a ship have rotted on the sea, then fungi, as it were, break out upon them first, in which in course of time one may discern evident forms of birds, which afterwards are clothed with feathers, and at last become alive and fly.

However, there is a problem with this admittedly entertaining theory – apart, that is, from it being biologically impossible. According to the *OED*, the first reference to 'barnacle' relating to the bird goes back to the early thirteenth century, whereas it was not used (in print, at least) for the crustacean until the 1570s.

Intriguingly, the medieval church decreed that because barnacle geese were 'neither flesh, nor born of flesh', they could be eaten on fast days when consuming meat (though not, for some reason, fish) was prohibited.

To me, this sounds like a convenient way of getting around the dietary rules of Christianity. Certainly, those in high places were not convinced: the thirteenth-century Holy Roman

Emperor Frederick II closely examined a goose barnacle and found no sign of anything birdlike about them.

Geese have also featured in several traditional children's stories, the best-known being 'Mother Goose'. This benevolent character first appears in English in the early eighteenth century – not long before 'The Twelve Days of Christmas'. Like that carol, it was originally written down in French, in this case by the pioneer of fairy tales, Charles Perrault. An esteemed member of the highbrow Académie Française, Perrault also rewrote many other classic folk-tales for children, including 'Little Red Riding Hood', 'Cinderella', 'Puss in Boots' and 'The Sleeping Beauty', and was a major influence on the German Brothers Grimm.

The other celebrated goose-based story is that of the goose that laid the golden egg. Going back all the way to *Aesop's Fables* (thought to have been written around the sixth or seventh century BC), this morality tale warns the reader not to become so greedy that they destroy the source of their good fortune. Ironically, this ancient fable is even more relevant now, in the Age of the Anthropocene, when we as human beings seem hell-bent on destroying the very planet on which our existence depends.

Two modern works of literature – one fiction, the other non-fiction – have been inspired by a North American species, the snow goose. The first and best-known is Paul Gallico's *The Snow Goose*. This started life as a short story that appeared in the US magazine the *Saturday Evening Post* in 1940, and had such a positive response from readers that the author expanded it into a novella, which was published in April 1941.

The Snow Goose tells the story of a disabled artist, Philip

Rhayader, living a solitary life on the coast of Essex, who meets a young local girl called Fritha. The two befriend one another when Fritha rescues a wounded snow goose, lost and stranded thousands of miles from its native home.

Later, despite his disabilities, Rhayader responds to the emergency call for privately-owned boats to head across the sea to Dunkirk, to rescue the thousands of British servicemen stranded there. But he never returns, and the goose comes to symbolise his soul, and Fritha's lost (and unrequited) love for him. The book gained even greater fame when it was turned into a BBC-TV film in 1971, starring Richard Harris as Rhayader and Jenny Agutter as Fritha.

Six decades after Gallico's story first appeared, in 2002, a young writer called William Fiennes wrote a prizewinning book, *The Snow Geese*. Fiennes followed wild snow geese from their winter home in Texas to their breeding grounds on Baffin Island, in the remote Canadian Arctic. As in Gallico's story, the geese were used symbolically; in this case as a meditation on the importance of home to the traveller.

The use of wild geese as a symbol of freedom is, perhaps, down to the sheer wonder we feel when we watch flocks of migrating birds passing overhead each spring and autumn. They mark the passing of the seasons, yet they also symbolise how life comes back full circle over time; a parable of the ability of life to constantly renew itself.

Both of these literary works also remind us that 'wild geese', particularly when they manifest in large, noisy and spectacular gatherings, exert a mysterious pull on many of us. This is especially true of a man who was arguably the greatest conservationist who ever lived: Sir Peter Scott. During his long and distinguished life, Scott was never out of the public eye: even as a child he was known to the British public, as the forlorn young boy who had never known his father, the polar explorer Robert Falcon Scott, 'Scott of the Antarctic'. Captain Scott tragically perished with his colleagues when just a few miles from safety, after losing a desperate race with the Norwegian explorer Roald Amundsen to be the first to reach the South Pole, in 1911. The young Peter was just two years old. Famously, and to the eternal gratitude of all who love the natural world, Captain Scott wrote in his last letter home to his wife Kathleen, 'Make the boy interested in natural history if you can; it is better than games.'

Initially, however, the young Peter Scott spent more time shooting birds than conserving them. In a chapter in his best-selling autobiography, *The Eye of the Wind*, published in 1961, Scott described his overwhelming excitement at shooting his very first goose – a bean goose – in North Norfolk, at the age of eighteen.

There is a popular myth about Scott that suggests that soon afterwards, before the outbreak of the Second World War (in which he would play a distinguished part as a naval officer), he shot a goose that fell wounded, out of reach on the mud. He is supposed to have watched it, helpless, as it struggled and eventually died. This led, the story goes, to a 'road to Damascus' conversion on his part, after which he never picked up a gun again.

There is only one problem with this touching tale: it is utter nonsense. In fact, Scott continued to shoot geese and other

Goose

wildfowl well into the 1950s, long after he had founded the now world-famous Wildfowl and Wetlands Trust at Slimbridge on the Severn estuary. Elsewhere in *The Eye of the Wind*, he defended himself against accusations of cruelty:

> If anyone asked me, and they frequently did, how I could equate the killing with my evident love of the living birds, my answer was given without hesitation. They were man's traditional quarry and it was part of man's instinct to hunt; it was part of the birds' instinct to be hunted.

To be fair to Peter Scott, he arguably did more not just for geese, but for all the world's wildlife, than virtually any other human being, before or since. As well as the WWT, he also co-founded the World Wildlife Fund (WWF, now the World Wide Fund for Nature) and, more or less single-handedly, saved the world's rarest species of goose, the Nene (also known as the Hawaiian goose) from extinction. With the wild population down to just thirty individuals by the early 1950s, Scott knew that drastic action had to be taken, so he bred these charming little birds at Slimbridge, and later returned them to the wild.

But perhaps the greatest evidence for his lifelong love of geese is their constant appearance in his many paintings of wildlife, which perfectly evoke the experience of a flock of geese passing overhead, uttering their unmistakeable, haunting calls.

Seven Swans A-Swimming

MUTE SWANS

When it came to choosing birds for 'The Twelve Days of Christmas', the swan must have been an obvious candidate. Swans are not only the largest British bird; they are also one of the best-known and best-loved. They mate for life, and in many cultures are said to symbolise purity, love and fidelity.

More prosaically, 'swans a-swimming' have long been used as a metaphor for something that appears calm and serene on the surface, but with frantic activity going on out of sight – based on the way swans appear to glide limpidly along a river, while their feet are presumably hard at work paddling just beneath the water.

Swans are the subject of countless myths and legends, from the Ancient Greek story of Leda and the Swan to Tchaikovsky's famous ballet, *Swan Lake*. There are many urban myths about swans, too. Some say they are completely silent – yet they are not; others believe that they all belong to the Queen – even though they don't. It is also commonly believed that a single blow of a swan's wing can break a man's arm – it can't, though that hefty beak can do some damage if you get too close! These very different ways of looking at the same bird point to the rather ambivalent nature of swans: at the same time serene, beautiful creatures and rather elemental, even violent ones.

What is obvious to even the casual observer is that swans are big – very big. A large male can reach a length of more than 150 cm (about 60 inches) from beak to tail, and weigh up to 13 kilograms (28 lbs). That's more than 2,500 times the weight of Britain's smallest bird, the goldcrest. Mute swans also lay the largest egg of any British bird: at 300 grams (11 ounces) it is about six times heavier than a typical hen's egg. And swans also have more feathers than any other bird in the world: an incredible total of 25,000.

Mute swans, with their characteristic black-and-orange bill, are just one of three species of swan found in Britain. The other two, whooper and Bewick's, are often known as 'wild swans', and are both winter visitors here from their breeding grounds to the north and east. Both have black-and-yellow bills, but differ considerably in size: the Bewick's being noticeably smaller than either whooper or mute swans.

Although we may think we know everything there is to know about the mute swan, this species still has the power to surprise. Few people are aware that, until relatively recently, swans were widely regarded as domesticated, rather than wild birds; indeed, until the late eighteenth century, their official name was 'tame swan'. One Victorian ornithologist, the Scot William MacGillivray, even went as far as to claim that 'there is no evidence of its ever having been shot or caught, in a truly wild state, in any part of Britain.'

Even as late as 1895, W. H. Hudson could still write about the mute swan as if it were a feral species, hardly different from its domesticated cousins:

> The mute, or tame swan, is as well known to most people as the turkey, goose, and pheasant, and, like the pheasant, is supposed to be a foreign species . . . As a semi-domestic species it exists throughout the British Islands, but whether wild birds of this species visit us or not is not known, since wild and semi-wild birds are indistinguishable.

As a result of this attitude, our understanding of the mute swan's historical status is hazy at best. One legend suggests that Richard I (Richard the Lionheart) brought mute swans back from the Crusades at the end of the twelfth century. But digging down into the archaeological evidence, we can be confident that the species was present much earlier than this.

Generations of our ancestors would no doubt have killed these birds for food. Then, from the Anglo-Saxon period onwards, swans were captured and domesticated, and prevented from escaping by having their wings clipped (or 'pinioned') to render them more or less flightless.

At some stage, soon after the Norman Conquest, the swan was declared a royal bird. This was partly a symbolic gesture – a nod to the swan's regal bearing – but also a very practical one: by claiming ownership over these large and tasty birds, the Crown was able to reserve them for royal feasts. One popular way of serving

Swan

swan was to stuff it with the carcasses of eight other birds, in descending order of size: goose, duck, mallard, chicken, pheasant, partridge, pigeon and woodcock. Hopefully this managed to disguise the taste of the swan – said to be rather like 'fishy mutton'.

Today, it is often said that all swans belong to the Queen, but the truth is rather more complicated than that. The Crown does technically have some rights over any unmarked swans in open water, but the vast majority of swans in Britain no longer have 'owners', and are subject to the same wild bird protection laws as any other species.

There is one important exception to this rule: on the River Thames, the ownership of swans is shared between the Crown and two other ancient institutions from the City of London, the Vintners' and Dyers' Livery Companies. These were founded in the twelfth and fifteenth centuries to control the sale of wine and cloth, but today work mainly as charitable organisations.

Every July, representatives from all three bodies gather on the Thames to round up the swans and mark them, in a 900-year-old tradition known as 'swan-upping'.

I was brought up a stone's throw from the River Thames at Shepperton, and recall being taken as a child to witness this ancient ceremony. We gathered one bright summer's morning at Shepperton Lock, location of the Monty Python 'fish-slapping dance' sketch. We had arrived early, to ensure that we had a good view of the proceedings. But as time went by, with no sign of the swan-uppers, we were beginning to get bored and restless. Then, without warning, a group of gentlemen emerged from the riverside pub, boarded their skiffs, and swiftly vanished out of sight around a bend in the river. They – and the swans – never reappeared.

I later learned that swan-upping involves catching each swan, and checking marks on its bill to work out which of the three groups is the rightful owner. The marking used to be done by cutting a series of marks into the birds' beaks – a rather barbaric practice, now long discontinued. This explains the peculiar name of one of the City of London's former coaching inns, which closed in the 1860s: The Swan with Two Necks. This is thought to be a linguistic corruption of 'two nicks' – a reference to the way the birds were marked. Today, a ring with the relevant information is simply attached to the swan's leg.

In many ways, though, we are fortunate there are any swans to be 'upped' at all. By the start of Queen Victoria's reign, in 1837, the practice of keeping swans had gone into terminal decline, and the species was in real trouble. Fortunately, from the early twentieth century onwards, illegal poaching became less of a problem, and numbers started to rise.

Today, the mute swan is common and widespread throughout most of lowland Britain. As the ornithologist David Bannerman noted, more than sixty years ago, 'wherever one may be in rural England, a pair of them is almost sure to be in possession of the village pond or nearby lake.'

However, the species is not spread equally through Britain. It is largely absent from upland areas like the Scottish Highlands, Pennines, Snowdonia and the high ground of Dartmoor and Exmoor. Estimates suggest that there are roughly 6,000 breeding pairs, along with almost 20,000 non-breeding birds, making about 32,000 birds in all.

The population appears to be fairly stable, having hardly changed at all since the first BTO *Atlas* survey from 1968-72. However, in recent years the species has managed to expand its range northwards, colonising Shetland in the early 1990s. There it can sometimes be seen nesting alongside its cousin from the north, the whooper swan, which during the same period extended its own range south from Iceland to Shetland.

Elsewhere in the world, mute swans can be found across a broad swathe of northern and central Europe: from Ireland in the west, to Turkey and the Caucasus in the east, and in parts of Asia. But the picture is muddied by the way the species has been introduced across much of the globe, including North America, Japan, Australia and New Zealand.

There is also now a growing feral population of the black swan in Britain, including a flock once kept by Winston Churchill on the lake of his home at Chartwell, Kent. Originally from Australia, this conspicuous bird has been deliberately released or escaped from captivity for the past 150 years or more, and may be on the brink of forming a self-sustaining population here. If so, it could soon join the Canada goose and ring-necked parakeet as an official British bird.

Swans are a very familiar sight around my home on the Somerset Levels, where extensive marshes, reedbeds, ditches and drains support one of the largest and densest populations in the whole of the country. Whenever I visit Noah's Lake, a shallow area of open water on the Avalon Marshes, I regularly count well over a hundred swans, while smaller flocks, numbering a score or more

birds, frequently gather on the grassy fields around our village to graze.

A pair of swans breeds in most years along the lane that runs by the back of my home. They typically raise up to half a dozen cygnets, though not all survive to adulthood. I occasionally come across broods of seven or eight young, while the most I have seen was a party of ten well-grown cygnets, still accompanied by their parents, almost a year after they first hatched. Other locations where large numbers of swans are found include the East Anglian Broads and Fens and, more surprisingly, offshore islands such as North and South Uist in the Outer Hebrides.

One of the world's largest gatherings of mute swans is at Abbotsbury Swannery in Dorset, thought to have been founded by Benedictine monks in the twelfth century, where there are over 600 birds, including about 150 breeding pairs. The swannery was originally set up at this location because of the area's unusual geology. Some time towards the end of the last Ice Age, about 12,000 years ago, a shallow lagoon was formed behind the long stretch of shingle, Chesil Beach, that runs along the Dorset coast. Known today as the Fleet Lagoon, at a length of 13 km (just over eight miles) it is the longest in Europe. This brackish waterbody provides the ideal habitat for the swans: shelter from the worst of the weather, plus plenty of food.

What is odd about Abbotsbury Swannery is how these normally highly territorial birds are able to nest side-by-side in such close proximity. It seems their usual instincts have been overridden by the great safety of nesting together, and especially the daily provision of food, which is handed out every afternoon in a mass feeding spectacle, attracting thousands of visitors.

Swans are now so common a presence in our lives that many birders rarely stop to take a good look at them, let alone study their behaviour. That's a pity, as swans have a fascinating lifestyle, with some specific adaptations, many a product of their large size.

For example, that long, curved neck isn't just for show. It allows the swan to feed at a greater depth than other surface-feeding waterbirds like dabbling ducks; and by 'up-ending' it is able to reach even deeper into the water, to feed on its staple diet of aquatic vegetation. Yet swans are not strictly vegetarian, being partial to the occasional frog, toad and fish to vary their diet.

As such a large and dominant bird, it might be thought that swans face few dangers. Yet, like all birds that nest by the edge of lakes, ponds and rivers, they are very vulnerable to predation from foxes, though they do manage to defend themselves and their chicks against most attackers. A far more serious and insidious threat comes from poisoning by lead shot (and, until they were banned, lead weights used by anglers).

A more positive development is the creation of new wetland habitats, such as disused reservoirs, gravel pits and, in my area of Somerset, peat-diggings, which has provided more room for both breeding and wintering birds. So the future of the mute swan, for the moment at least, appears to be secure.

*

Swans are well-known to mate for life, unlike most other birds, so have long been a symbol of constancy and fidelity. Yet in the Greek myth of Leda and the Swan, Helen of Troy is said to have been conceived when Zeus, disguised as a swan, seduced Leda, the Queen of Sparta. I say seduced, but really this borders on rape, especially as depicted by the poet W. B. Yeats:

> A sudden blow: the great wings beating still
> Above the staggering girl, her thighs caressed
> By the dark webs, her nape caught in his bill,
> He holds her helpless breast upon his breast.

This curious subject, which seems so far removed from our usual image of the calm, faithful swan (the subject, indeed, of another Yeats poem, 'The Wild Swans at Coole'), was also tackled by some of the greatest artists of the Renaissance, including Leonardo da Vinci, whose painting was never actually completed, even though he made several preliminary drawings, and Michelangelo, whose work appears to have been destroyed. During the twentieth century, the artist Paul Cézanne, poet W. B. Yeats, and songwriter Lou Reed also featured the myth in their work.

As Mark Cocker wryly noted in his mammoth tome on the cultural history of birds around the world, *Birds and People*, 'For some largely inexplicable reason, this affair between the swan god and Leda seems to have haunted Western artists (largely male artists, it must be said) like few other divine one-night stands.' This is perhaps, as he suggested, because it breaks the taboo of inter-species mating. Others have suggested that, while it would have been highly offensive to depict a woman having sex with a man, for some reason this avian-human encounter was considered acceptable.

Yet the violent image of a woman being forcibly mated by a swan still retains the power to shock. As recently as 2012, the Metropolitan Police raided an art gallery in London's Mayfair and asked for an artwork on the subject to be removed – despite no members of the public having actually complained. It turned out that the only person to have been offended was a police officer who saw the painting in the gallery's window as he was passing by on a double-decker bus.

In other cultures, Norse mythology claims that swans are white because they drank pure water from a well in the kingdom of the gods; while in Hinduism, swans represent the harmony between the material and spiritual worlds, because they live in both air and water. Swans even figure in the night sky: the constellation Cygnus, usually seen in the northern hemisphere in summer and autumn, is based on a legend about a swan: 'Cygnus' being the swan's scientific name.

In medieval times, the twelfth-century St Hugh of Lincoln formed a very close bond with a swan, which is said to have taken food from his hand and slept in his bedroom, and was by his bedside when he died. He later became the patron saint of sick children.

More recently, the famous design on the Swan Vestas matchbox was based on a black-and-white photograph by the pioneering bird photographer Eric Hosking. As Hosking recalled in his autobiography, *An Eye for a Bird*, early on in his career he was contacted by an advertising agency asking for a photograph of a swan. Realising he had nothing suitable on file, he cycled to a North London park where he knew he could get close to the birds:

> With one hand I cast my bread upon the waters and, as the swans approached, worked the shutter of the reflex with the other. As soon as I felt sure that one, at least, of the shots would be suitable I rushed home, developed the negatives, made prints while the plates were still wet, and posted them that evening.
>
> One of these pictures appeared shortly after on hoardings all over the country. A drawing made from my photograph has been the Swan Vesta sign ever since.

Swans have entered the English language, too, in many words and phrases. We talk of someone 'swanning about', when they go on an aimless journey, or simply wander around, as in the actor Dirk Bogarde's acid observation that a woman 'swanned about at the party like the Queen Mother'.

The word 'swansong' alludes to the widespread and persistent belief that, as it is dying, the swan sings a haunting song. This idea appears in the writings of Aristotle and Pliny, who wrote that 'These birds are wont to sing even when just about to die.' How, why and where this myth arose is a mystery: there is no actual evidence that dying swans make any sound at all. Perhaps it relates to the frequent idea that birds are the repositories of the souls of dead people – a concept Plato called 'metempsychosis'.

Nevertheless, the myth persisted: it can be found in the works of Chaucer and Shakespeare (dubbed the 'Swan of Avon' by Ben Jonson), who in his long poem 'The Rape of Lucrece' wrote:

> And now this pale Swan in her watery nest,
> Begins the sad dirge of her certain ending.

In response, the nineteenth-century poet Samuel Taylor Coleridge coined this witty couplet:

> Swans sing before they die; 'twere no bad thing,
> Should certain persons die before they sing.

The myth of the dying swan reached its apogee in Tchaikovsky's ballet *Swan Lake*, based on a German fairy-tale, which tells the story of a princess who has been turned into a swan by a sorcerer's curse. She is condemned to spend every day as a swan, swimming on a lake made entirely of tears, and her nights as a human being, isolated from her peers. The conclusion, in which both the princess and her suitor die, is widely considered one of the most moving of any theatrical performance.

However, one quirky ornithological question does arise. Given that the composer was Russian, it is surely most likely that the species referred to was either the whooper or Bewick's swan, both of which breed widely across northern Russia, and would have been familiar to Tchaikovsky. The Finnish composer Sibelius also adapted the haunting call of whooper swans – inspired, apparently, by witnessing sixteen of them in flight one day – as one of the musical motifs in his celebrated Fifth Symphony.

Perhaps the best-known story about swans is Hans Christian Andersen's *The Ugly Duckling*. This perennial fairy-tale was first published in Danish in 1843, and soon translated into many other languages, including English. Clearly an allegory about personal transformation, the story struck a chord with children and adults alike, and has been turned into an opera, a musical, and Walt Disney's animated film.

There is also Danny Kaye's famous song, written for the Disney film by Frank Loesser, with the witty but inappropriate quacking soundtrack, in which the eponymous bird is first drummed out of town by the other birds, and then, following a winter hiding away in shame, is transformed into a fine-looking, snow-white swan.

In Hans Christian Andersen's native Denmark, the original tale of *The Ugly Duckling* is so well-loved that, in 1984, the mute

swan was named as the country's national bird, supplanting the original holder of that title, the skylark.

Amongst all this myth and legend, it can be hard to pin down the facts about this imposing and impressive bird. Even the name is misleading: as we have seen, the species was originally known as the 'tame swan', but as the practice of keeping domesticated swans declined this was increasingly regarded as unsuitable. So, in 1785, the name 'mute swan' was coined by the ornithologist Thomas Pennant, one of Gilbert White's two correspondents in *The Natural History of Selborne*. The name derives from the fact that, unlike its cousins, the mute swan does not usually call in flight.

It is true that, especially compared with the whooper swan and its two North American relatives, the trumpeter and whistling swans (all named after their call), the mute swan is indeed relatively quiet. The neck shapes of the different species are a clue to the sounds they make: whoopers have a very long, straight neck, while mutes have a curved one, making it harder for them to emit loud sounds while airborne.

However, the mute swan does make a variety of honking, whistling and hissing sounds (the Russian name for the species, *bezglasnyy lebed*, derives from a word meaning 'hissing'). Most notably, when mute swans fly overhead, their wings make a 'hushing sound', memorably described by the US writer Paul Theroux as sounding like two people making love in a hammock. In their book *The Mute Swan*, Mike Birkhead and Christopher Perrins speculated that this curious sound, unique amongst the world's seven species of swan, helps keep the birds together in flight, especially when travelling at night.

Swans are, indeed, as faithful as the myths and legends suggest: occasionally a pair will split up, but normally they only do so when one dies, and the survivor takes up with a new mate. Their fidelity may be admirable, but it results in some of the greatest aggression shown by any bird to intruders near their nest, with some battles between rival males fought to the death.

As William Yarrell noted in 1843:

The male has frequently been styled 'the peaceful monarch of the lake', but . . . pending the season of incubation, and rearing the young, there is scarcely any bird more pugnacious . . . he is in reality a bird to be feared and avoided by all that inhabit his watery domain, for he drives his weaker subjects in all directions.

Having built a large and bulky nest, usually in a ditch or along the edge of a pond, lake or river, and often in full view, the female lays between four and seven eggs – occasionally more – and incubates them for between five and seven weeks. Born 'precocial', the cygnets are are able to feed and swim almost immediately. However, they remain with their parents for months afterwards, and even a year after hatching still show patches of grey in their white plumage. They do not breed until they are four years old, which is why in summer they gather in large, loose flocks, like bored teenagers hanging around in the local park.

Typically, mute swans live to about the age of ten, but the oldest recorded wild individual was almost thirty years old.

Causes of death are varied and numerous, but collisions with power lines (and, latterly, wind turbines) make up the largest single factor – though that may be because those caught and killed by foxes, for example, are harder to find.

There can be no doubt that, of all Britain's birds, few are held in quite such affection amongst the public as the mute swan. If you need convincing, just consider that 'The Swan' is the fifth commonest of the 58,000 or so pub names in Britain and Ireland, and by far the highest-ranking bird. Along with my local gastropub, The Swan in Wedmore, another famous example is The Swan, in the village of Clare, south of Bury St Edmunds in Suffolk. This has a complex carved swan above its doors, dating back to the fifteenth century and said to be the oldest pub sign in Britain. The pub's longevity confirms what we have already suspected: that of all the birds in this book, it is swans with which we perhaps feel the closest connection.

Eight Maids A-Milking

NIGHTJARS

On a fine, warm midsummer evening, as dusk begins to fall, a strange, rather mechanical sound floats across a Dorset heath. At first, it seems easy to pinpoint the bird's location; moments later, however, it appears to have flown further away across the gorse-strewn valley; then, nearer again.

Yet this unseen singer has not moved at all: it is simply turning its head from side-to-side, to achieve a ventriloquial effect. The creature making this bizarre sound is one of the most secretive and enigmatic of all our birds: the nightjar.

It may not be obvious why I have chosen the nightjar as the avian equivalent of the 'eight maids a-milking'. Other suggestions included the blue tit, because for a few decades in the mid-to-late twentieth century, blue tits were notorious for the clever trick they had learned of pecking into the foil tops of milk bottles left on doorsteps by the milkman to get at the cream. But for me, a myth linking the nightjar with the sucking of one of our more esoteric farmyard animals is the clincher – more on this in a moment.

The nightjar is undoubtedly a very charismatic and unusual bird. In what was for him an uncharacteristically poetic passage, the Victorian ornithologist William MacGillivray wrote:

It is evening; the ruddy streaks of the western sky have faded into a dull purple; the moon already in the heavens sends abroad her pale light; there is silence in the woods . . . how soothing [is] . . . the placid quiet, the balmy air, and the faint light of this secluded place. Hark! It is the *whirr* of the Fern Owl. Again! Nearer, more distant, faint. It has ceased; but there, the creature itself sweeps overhead, glides along, flutters, shoots aside, and is off.

No modern writer has ever captured the character of this nocturnal bird better; perhaps because nowadays nature writing tends to focus its attention on species that are easier to find and see, and which reward the time-pressed twenty-first-century observer more easily for their efforts. Our distinguished ancestors seem to have been far more familiar with the nightjar than most of us are today.

Officially known as the European nightjar, the species living in Britain is about the size and weight of a blackbird. It has long, pointed wings, a large mouth surrounded by bristles which help it detect insects when hunting, and cryptically patterned plumage, so that the bird can rest unseen on the ground (often amongst leaf-litter) during the day, without being detected.

In the early nineteenth century, the poet John Clare regularly observed nightjars on Emmonsailes Heath, near his Northamptonshire home, as shown by this wonderfully free-flowing passage from one of his *Natural History Letters*:

One cannot pass over a wild heath in a summer evening without being stopt to listen and admire its novel and pleasing noise . . . it is a beautiful mottld bird variously shadowd with the colors of black and brown . . . its eye is keen its bill hookshapd and its mouth very wide with long bristle like hairs growing at each corner.

Clare generally used one old name for the bird – fern owl – but his predecessor Gilbert White, writing half a century earlier, preferred the name that links the nightjar with our Christmas carol: the goatsucker, as in this passage from *The Natural History of Selborne*:

There is no bird, I believe, whose manners I have studied more than the *caprimulgus* (the GOATSUCKER) as it is a wonderful and curious creature . . . It perches usually on a bare twig, with its head lower than its tail . . . The bird is most punctual in beginning its song exactly at the close of day; so exactly, that I have known it to strike up more than once or twice just as the report of the Portsmouth evening gun, which we can hear when the weather is still.

White was convinced – rightly – that the churring note of the nightjar is produced vocally (unlike, for example, the 'drumming' of the snipe, which uses its tail feathers). He recalled one occasion when he and some neighbours were in a small straw building, and a nightjar came and perched on the roof. As it called, it 'gave a sensible vibration to the whole building!' He also wrote this striking phrase, using both folk-names for the bird: 'fern-owls, or goat-suckers, glance in the dark over the tops of trees like a meteor.'

Living in rural Hampshire – still a key stronghold for the species – White had plenty of opportunities for regular encounters with the nightjar:

> On the twelfth of July I had a fair opportunity of contemplating the motions of the *Caprimulgus*, or fern-owl, as it was playing around a large oak that swarmed with fern-chafers [cockchafers]. The powers of its wing were wonderful, exceeding, if possible, the various evolutions and quick turns of the swallow genus . . . I saw it distinctly, more than once, put out its short leg while on the wing, and, by a bend of its head, deliver somewhat into its mouth.

White went on to speculate that this behaviour was the origin of the nightjar's peculiar serrated middle claw, though others, including William Yarrell, suggested this might be used to rid the bird's plumage of parasites, or to comb the hairs or bristles around its bill. Another Victorian nature writer, Edward Stanley, Bishop of Norwich, claimed that the claw was elongated so the bird could carry its eggs to a more secure spot if disturbed.

Given that Stanley also believed that eagles carry off small children, and other nonsense, it is hardly surprising that Yarrell's is the correct interpretation: the bird does indeed use this unusually long claw to preen its feathers and remove troublesome parasites.

Nightjars emerge at dusk to feed, on flies, dragonflies and even glow-worms, but primarily on moths and beetles, as Thomas Bewick noted: 'It is a great destroyer of the cock-chafer or dor-beetle, from which circumstance, in some places, it is called the Dor-Hawk.' One modern nature poet, the ornithologist Mike Toms, has coined the alternative name 'moth-gobbler' for this voracious bird.

According to Lewis R. Loyd, writing in the 1920s at Nidderdale in the Yorkshire Dales, nightjars were called 'gabble-ratchets', and were thought to be 'the souls of unbaptised infants doomed to wander forever in the air'. Gabble comes from a word meaning 'corpse', and was also given to other nocturnal birds, including migrating geese. Elsewhere, in Cheshire and Shropshire, the local name was 'lich fowl', which also means corpse, an association presumably made because of the nightjar's nocturnal habits.

More than a score of local names (quite a lot, given that the bird itself is so elusive) include a dozen based on its call – eve-jar, razor grinder and screech hawk among them; and several based on its appearance – night hawk, night crow and night swallow. The name 'nightjar', which first appears in English in 1630, and was finally adopted as the official name in 1843, is a corruption of 'night-churr', referring to the bird's distinctive call. It may sound like a continuous stream of sound, but it is in fact a series of very rapid individual notes, produced at a rate of between 30 and 40 times a second.

But of all the folk-names for the nightjar, the most puzzling is surely the one that Gilbert White himself preferred: 'goatsucker'. The name is a direct translation of the Classical Latin *Caprimulgus* (the nightjar's generic and family name), from *capra* (meaning 'she-goat') and *mulgere* ('to milk'). The word 'goatsucker' first appeared in English in 1611, in a dictionary of the French

and English languages, and was also used by Ray and Willughby (1678), Thomas Pennant (1768) and as recently as 2001 in a reference to a bird in Australia. It has direct equivalents in several European names for the nightjar, including those in German, Italian, Spanish and Polish.

Its use goes back to the earliest writings on birds, by the Greek philosopher Aristotle. Writing in the fourth century BC, he confidently asserted that 'Flying to the udders of she-goats, [the nightjar] sucks them.' The Roman philosopher Pliny the Elder, writing in the first century AD, perpetuated the myth:

Those called goat-suckers . . . enter the shepherds' stalls and fly to the goats' udders in order to suck their milk, which injures the udder and makes it perish, and the goats they have milked in this way gradually go blind.

William MacGillivray expanded on these classical references, explaining that 'The ancients accused it of injuring the teats of goats in its attempts to milk them, and thus it received the names of *Caprimulgus* and *Aegotheles*, which, having been translated into the modern tongues, it retains at the present day.' He also wryly noted that 'the extreme absurdity of the name . . . seems to be its best recommendation.' He was quite right: yet sadly this misplaced belief led to nightjars being vilified and even persecuted for a crime they had not actually committed.

So how did this longstanding belief come into being? It does indeed derive from the bird's nocturnal feeding habits, but the nightjar is not stealing milk: rather seizing flying insects which have concentrated around domestic livestock – including goats. This explanation was first proposed by J. E. Harting, in his readable and informative book *Our Summer Migrants*, published in 1875:

> Cattle, as they graze in the evening, disturb numerous moths and flies, and the Nightjar, unalarmed by the animals, to whose presence it becomes accustomed, dashes boldly down to seize a moth which is hovering round their feet, or a fly which has settled on the udder. Being detected in this act by unobservant persons, the story has gone forth that the Goatsucker steals the milk.

The mystery of the goatsucker myth may have been cleared up more than a century ago, yet the nightjar continues to mystify and surprise us. Whether or not the anonymous composer of 'The Twelve Days of Christmas' was thinking about nightjars when he wrote the line 'eight maids a-milking', is perhaps a moot point. But given that he would have been familiar with the goatsucker story, I like to think he was.

Nightjars, along with their American counterparts the night-hawks, potoos and oilbird, and the Australasian owlet-nightjars and frogmouths, are generally placed in their own distinctive order: Caprimulgiformes (also named after their supposed goat-milking habits). This traditionally comes between the owls (Strigiformes) and Swifts (Apodiformes).

There are roughly eighty species of 'typical nightjars', found across six of the world's seven continents, being absent from Antarctica (as well as the Arctic and New Zealand). Given that most are so tricky to see, it's not surprising that several other species are named after their peculiar calls, including the chuck-will's-widow and whip-poor-will, both found in the USA and southern parts of Canada.

A few species have variations on the typical body-shape, in-cluding the pennant-winged and standard-winged nightjars of Equatorial Africa, the males of which sport a single, hugely elongated feather on each wing, which they use to impress the females during courtship displays.

Nightjars and their allies are highly adaptable. They are able to live in deserts, in jungles, and even in large cities, where they take advantage of artificial lighting (such as floodlights on sports grounds or at airports) to feed on flying insects, including thou-sands of moths attracted to these night-time illuminations.

They can also enter a state of torpor during cold weather: indeed, one North American species, the common poorwill, does not migrate, but instead goes into a period of hibernation during the winter months, lowering its body temperature and more or less shutting down its metabolism to survive without food.

Some nightjars are very rare, with a highly restricted range; none more so than the Nechisar nightjar, which so far is only known from a single wing found in a remote part of Ethiopia in 1990, and has never been seen alive, before or since. But of all the various species, the European nightjar is the most widespread, being found across a broad swathe of temperate Europe, North Africa and western Asia, from Ireland and Portugal in the west to Lake Baikal in the east.

In Britain, the nightjar is largely a bird of open areas dotted with bushes and trees: notably the lowland heaths of southern England (especially Dorset and Hampshire) and more recently conifer plantations.

For much of the twentieth century, the British nightjar population was suffering a slow but steady fall in numbers. In common with many other insectivorous species, this was because of a combination of the loss of habitat to farming and development, and a general decline in large flying insects, especially the larger moths.

Yet recently, the species has, perhaps surprisingly, reversed this trend: the number of churring males has more than doubled in the past few decades, from just over 2,000 in 1981 to roughly

4,600 today. This is partly a result of climate change, allowing the nightjar to extend its range northwards, and to maintain a foothold in southern Scotland.

Another reason for the rise in numbers is that changes in the way we grow coniferous forests have created entirely new habitats for the species. Until the late twentieth century, most forestry plantations were uniform monocultures, in which all the trees were planted at the same time and then, once they had grown to the correct height, felled simultaneously. But conservationists within the forestry industry realised that by planting and harvesting the trees in rotation, they could create a mosaic of mini-habitats, rather than a monoculture. This was perfect for nightjars, which like so many other bird species thrive on a variety of habitats. However, optimism about the nightjar's recent growth in numbers must be offset by continued declines on the edge of its range, in Wales and especially in Ireland, where it is now almost extinct.

Nightjars are long-distance migrants, returning here from their winter quarters in sub-Saharan Africa in late April or early May, and remaining until August or September (though the males usually stop churring by the middle of July). The best chance of seeing – or at least hearing – them is on a warm, muggy evening in late May or June, on a southern lowland heath such as Town Common on the edge of Christchurch in Dorset, or the RSPB reserve at Arne.

Twenty years or more ago, I visited the former location with Bill Oddie and a film crew, to try to capture this mysterious bird on video. We had been told that the best way to see the males was to listen out for when their constant churring stops, and you hear their strange 'yipping' call, which indicates that the male has taken to the wing. At this point, you may also hear a snapping sound – the male's wings clapping against one another to attract a female.

Unbeknown to me, Bill had decided to test out a novel method of getting good views. So, as the male began to call, he whipped two clean white handkerchiefs out of his pocket and started to dance, simultaneously waving the hankies in the air. This is supposed to fool the bird into thinking that a rival male – whose wings have white patches near the tips, which are easily visible at night – is intruding into its territory. That night, despite Bill's best efforts at mimicking a Morris dancer, the ruse failed to work, but I have been assured that it usually does.

To see nightjars, you only have a short window of opportunity, an hour or so before and after dusk; for as soon as it becomes properly dark, they stop calling and head off to hunt. When abroad, especially in the tropics, I have often come across other species of nightjars sitting on the surface of roads after dark, which I always assumed was so they could warm up, using the stored heat rising from the tarmac, before flying off to hunt. This may well be one reason. However, studies now suggest that because roads are more open than the surrounding areas, they also provide a good platform from which the nightjars can look out for emerging insects.

Nightjars mainly forage in what Graham Martin, author of *Birds by Night*, calls 'open airspace'. You might imagine this would make studying them easier than, say, nocturnal forest-dwellers such as the tawny owl. Yet, as Martin points out, we are still not sure whether nightjars catch their prey by targeting individual insects, or simply open their mouths wide and trawl randomly through the night air like hopeful fishermen.

What we do know is that they take a very wide range of prey items, from tiny micro-moths and mosquitos to much larger beetles, moths and cockroaches. They are helped both by the sensitive bristles around their bill, and their very wide gape. Finally, they have one more secret weapon: a sensitive membrane on the roof of their mouth which, when struck by an insect, causes the gape to snap shut.

Unlike bats, nightjars do not use echolocation or any form of hearing to find their prey; instead, they rely on their keen eyesight. They have very large eyes relative to their size, a higher density of light-detecting rod cells, and another handy adaptation: a reflective layer behind the retina known as the *tapetum lucidum*, from the Latin meaning 'bright tapestry'.

This feature, revealed when a torchlight is directed at the bird (and shared with many nocturnal creatures, though not other birds), improves the nightjar's ability to detect light. It will not work in pitch darkness, but is especially helpful around dawn and dusk, or when the moon is shining. Any ambient light, however faint, helps nightjars spot their target prey in silhouette against the sky, while they will sometimes also take advantage of artificial light sources like floodlights. Like owls, after feeding they will regurgitate any indigestible food, such as the hard exoskeletons and wings of insects, in the form of pellets.

When male nightjars have attracted a mate, and settled down

to breed, they continue to call intermittently, usually at dusk, just before they head out to feed. Meanwhile, the female lays her two eggs – off-white, and liberally spotted and marbled with grey blotches – in a bare patch or scrape on the ground, in a gap between the vegetation. Female nightjars are more likely to lay their eggs in the period before the moon is full, which may be because when their chicks hatch, and the moon is waning, insects are more numerous and easier to catch.

Both the male and female take turns to sit tight on their precious clutch, incubating the eggs for about eighteen days. During this period, they rely on their camouflage to avoid predators, though they do still sometimes fall victim to snakes, crows and a range of mammals, including foxes, badgers, hedgehogs, stoats and weasels.

Once the young have hatched, they are fairly active, though they are still covered with down until they fledge, another eighteen or nineteen days later. By then, the female has often found another suitable spot to lay her second clutch of eggs – usually within 100 metres or so of the first – while the male looks after his original family, feeding them until they are just over a month old.

The French ornithologist Jacques Delamain wrote an account of a rarely seen family ritual of the species he called the 'winged wizard':

> Prompted by hunger, [the male] soars above the high wood, and makes off to the meadows where the little soft-bodied midsummer cockchafers fly about the poplar trees. Giddily looping and whirring he chases them . . . then, glutted for the moment, settles, inert, on the road. After a while he goes back to his mate and they and their young join together above the heath in a strange saraband – mad leaping and reeling, moth-like beating of wings, sinuous bat-like flights; and all the while the male clucks imperatively and claps his wing feathers.

Because most nightjars don't arrive back in Britain until mid-May, they need to get their two broods in as quickly as possible. The small number of nest records the BTO holds for the nightjar – just fifty-three – shows how tricky the nest can be to find.

A nightjar is even harder to spot during the day, when it will hide away to avoid disturbance and predators, often roosting horizontally along a branch, almost melting into the tree itself.

Or, if on the ground, it regularly turns its body to face the sun, to minimise any shadow.

Thomas Bewick, writing around 1800, noted that:

> In hot weather it is very fond of basking in the sun on the ground, and will suffer itself to be very nearly approached; but is difficult to be seen on account of the resemblance of its plumage to the colour of the place on which it chuses to sit.

J. E. Harting agreed that the nightjar is almost impossible to find during daylight hours, though he did recall stumbling across one 'asleep on the carriage drive within twenty yards of the house. The gravel was quite warm, and the bird was so loth to be disturbed that I almost succeeded in covering it with my hat before it took wing.' Nightjars are sometimes accidentally flushed during the day, as Harting also recalled: 'I have twice seen a keeper shoot one, exclaiming "There goes a Hawk!"'

In the authoritative masterwork *Birds of the Western Palearctic*, it is boldly stated that, because of the bird's nocturnal habits and cryptic plumage, seeing them at all 'is as much a matter of fortune as effort or knowledge'. That certainly applies to my very first sighting of a nightjar, back in July 1984, which even after more than thirty years remains my closest encounter with this enigmatic bird. And, unlike all my sightings since, it took place in broad daylight, on a bright, sunny afternoon.

I was walking across Westleton Heath, near Minsmere on the Suffolk coast, when I heard the unmistakable churring sound of a male nightjar. It seemed to be very close by, and coming from the dense, prickly foliage of a gorse bush; so I tentatively approached. As I did, a bizarre apparition rose up into the air like a vertical-take-off jet and, still churring, floated away across the heath on soft, noiseless wings. It was one of those encounters that, no matter how many years pass by, I shall never forget.

Along with the stories surrounding the name goatsucker, nightjars also feature strongly in other folklore and poetry. George Meredith, who wrote perhaps the best-known verse on birds in the English language, 'The Lark Ascending', referred to the nightjar in his long poem 'Love in the Valley', using a now-obsolete folk-name for the bird:

> Lone on the fir-branch, his rattle-note unvaried,
> Brooding o'er the gloom, spins the brown eve-jar.

Both William Wordsworth – 'The busy dor-hawk chases the white moth / With burring note' – and Thomas Hardy – 'If it be in the dusk when, like an eyelid's soundless blink, / The dew-fall-hawk comes crossing the shades to alight / Upon the wind-warped upland thorn' – also showed the breadth of their natural history knowledge when writing about the nightjar.

The Victorian nature-poet Mary Howitt made use of both English and American names for various nightjar species in her poem 'The Dor-Hawk':

> Fern-owl, Churn-owl, or Goat-sucker,
> Night-jar, Dor-hawk, or whate'er
> Be thy name among a dozen, –

Whip-poor-Will's and Who-are-you's cousin,
Chuck-Will's-widow's near relation,
Thou art at thy night vocation,
Thrilling the still evening air!

But the last word must go to the incomparable John Clare, whose sonnet 'The Fern Owl's Nest' uses the metre and syntax of his verse to capture the bird's peculiar jerky flight:

The weary woodman rocking home beneath
His tightly banded faggot wonders oft
While crossing over the furze-crowded heath
To hear the fern owls cry that whews aloft
In circling whirls and often by his head
Whizzes as quick as thought and ill and rest
As through the rustling ling with heavy tread
He goes nor heeds he tramples near its nest
That underneath the furze or squatting thorn
Lies hidden on the ground and teasing round
That lonely spot she wakes her jarring noise
To the unheeding waste till mottled morn
Fills the red East with daylight's coming sounds
And the heath's echoes mock the herding boys.

around the RSPB reserve of West Sedgemoor, are part of a major scheme to reintroduce this magnificent bird to the southwest of England, known as the Great Crane Project.

It all began in 2010, when the first batch of almost a hundred young cranes were released here, having been raised at the Wildfowl and Wetlands Trust's headquarters at Slimbridge in Gloucestershire. The eggs were brought to Britain from Germany, where the crane is still a common breeding bird, and the youngsters were reared in large enclosures, by staff dressed in 'crane costumes', to avoid the chicks becoming imprinted on human beings. Once they had grown to a reasonable size they were taken to Somerset, and eventually released into the wild.

Cranes would once have been found commonly across much of lowland Britain. In the early thirteenth century, King John (of Magna Carta fame) regularly hunted them, using the world's largest falcon, the gyr, to do so. We can gauge their abundance by looking at lists of the produce served at medieval feasts, such as that given at Cawood Castle in North Yorkshire in September 1465, to mark the enthronement of George Neville as Archbishop of York. To show the importance of himself and his family, Neville invited twenty-eight peers, fifty-nine knights, ten abbots, seven bishops and vast numbers of servants and hangerson – roughly 2,500 people altogether. All had to be fed and watered, and as well as vast numbers of oxen, chickens, pigs and other domestic animals, the inventory for this epic medieval blowout included the following wild birds: 400 swans, 400 herons, 204 bitterns, 200 pheasants, 500 partridges, 1,200 quails, 104 peacocks, 400 woodcocks, 100 curlews, 400 plovers, 2,400 ruffs, 4,000 mallard and teal, 1,000 egrets and last, but certainly not least, 204 cranes, all prepared, cooked and presented to the guests to be eaten.

Aside from the unimaginable expense, this early show of conspicuous consumption conveys crucial information about the abundance of waterbirds at that time. It also goes a long way to explaining why so many wetland species – including bitterns and egrets as well as cranes – ultimately disappeared from lowland England.

In what might seem to be an example of poetic justice, George Neville ultimately fell out of favour with King Edward IV. In 1472 he was arrested for treason and sent as a prisoner to Calais; two years later he returned home from exile, and died in disgrace in June 1476.

The other reason we know that cranes must have once been common and widespread throughout much of Britain is the number of place-names featuring the species. Glance at the map, and you'll find Cranbrook, Cranborne, Cranfield, Cranford, Cranham, Cranleigh, Cranmere, Cranwell and Cranwich, along with less obvious examples like Carnforth (meaning 'cranes' ford'), in Lancashire (whose railway station buffet was the location for the famous parting scene in David Lean's 1945 film *Brief Encounter*).

The frequency by which these names of villages and settlements appear has given rise to the suggestion that 'cran(e)' may in fact have been a synonym for 'heron'. However, given that we know cranes would have both bred in and migrated through Britain throughout our early history, it seems most likely that these place-names do indeed refer to the larger and grander species.

What is not in any doubt is that by the early sixteenth century cranes were on the verge of extinction as a British breeding bird. In 1534, Henry VIII passed a law preventing the eggs of any species of wildfowl being taken from March until June. Stealing a crane's egg was punished especially heavily: with the highest permitted penalty being a fine of twenty silver pennies, along with imprisonment.

But these punitive measures came too late: the last recorded successful breeding of cranes was at Hickling Broad, in north-east Norfolk, in June 1542. The death-knell for the crane appears to have been the rapid improvement of firearms, which allowed these shy birds to be shot more accurately, and from a greater distance, than before. Eggs and chicks were also regularly taken from the nest.

Being long-lived birds, cranes have a very low rate of reproduction, so they were especially vulnerable to pressures from hunting. Subsequently, the draining and development of their watery homes meant they were unable to return. When Elizabeth I visited Cambridgeshire in September 1577, she was served a feast including seventy bitterns, twenty-eight herons and twelve spoonbills – but just a single crane.

For the following 400 years, the crane was a rare but regular visitor to Britain, with roughly fifty records each year. These were birds migrating between their breeding grounds in Scandinavia and eastern Europe and their winter-quarters in France and Spain, which occasionally drifted off course due to easterly winds, and ended up on this side of the North Sea. From time to time, this might involve large flocks, most notably in late October and early November 1963, when bad weather on the near continent led to an influx of more than 500 cranes along the south coast of England.

But despite these regular visits, no-one could have predicted what would happen next. In autumn 1979, two young cranes turned up at Horsey in Norfolk, just a stone's throw from where the very last cranes had bred in Britain, back in the reign of King Henry VIII. Instead of moving on the following spring, they stayed; a year later, in 1981, they attempted to breed. Although they failed that first time, the following spring the pair success-fully hatched a single chick – the first wild crane to be born in Britain for more than four centuries.

For some years afterwards, as the flock of cranes gradually grew, it was suggested that the birds had been deliberately re-leased there, but this was based on an unfounded rumour. Over time, the population in Norfolk has risen slowly but steadily, and the birds are now a regular sight over this low-lying part of East Anglia. Indeed, this is where I first saw the species, on a chilly November day more than thirty years ago, when three cranes flew right past me, wings spread, necks extended, and uttering their unforgettable bugling call.

Given that since then, cranes have not only established them-selves in Norfolk, but have also bred in neighbouring Suffolk and Cambridgeshire, and further afield in Yorkshire and Scot-land, we might wonder why they needed to be reintroduced into Somerset at all. But as the WWT's Nigel Jarrett has explained, they might have taken hundreds of years to colonise south-west England under their own steam. Nor was the decision to bring

Duck and Crane.

back the birds taken lightly: only when studies had confirmed that a large enough area of restored wetland was available on the Somerset Levels, where the birds could establish a self-sustaining colony, did the project proceed.

The Great Crane Project, helped by the continued natural colonisation of wild cranes, has been a far greater success than even its most optimistic proponents would have imagined. In less than a decade, cranes have established themselves so well in Britain that a recent study suggested that within half a century there could be almost 300 breeding pairs of these majestic birds. The key to achieving this success, however, will be preserving and extending the wetlands on which they breed.

Incidentally, cranes have a long history in Somerset. In September 2018, the other key person behind the Great Crane Project, the RSPB's Damon Bridge, spent an afternoon on the muddy foreshore of the Severn estuary, at low tide. This part of our coastline has the second highest tidal span in the world (after the Bay of Fundy in Newfoundland), but Damon was still unprepared for what the receding waters would reveal: crane footprints dating back to roughly 8,000 years ago.

Crane footprints are very distinctive: three forward facing toes, spread out at an angle, and a single, rearward-facing toe at the back. This unmistakable shape resembled the symbol used on genealogical charts to show lines of descent or 'pedigree', meaning someone's ancestral lineage. This word in turn arose from the Anglo-Norman phrase *pé [pied] de grue*, meaning 'crane's foot'.

The 'common crane', as our familiar species is known, is one of fifteen members of its family, found mainly in the Old World, as well as North (but not South) America. They are all tall, long-legged and long-winged, and vary in size from the delicate demoiselle crane, which is less than a metre long, to the stately sarus crane of India, south-east Asia and parts of Australia which, at up to 175 cm (69 inches) in height, is the world's tallest flying bird.

Cranes of all species begin to pair up at two or three years old and, unless they persistently fail to breed successfully, usually stay together for life – as long as thirty, or even forty, years. That's why they have such an elaborate courtship, using both vocal and visual displays to maintain and strengthen the bond between the male and female.

One of the greatest bird spectacles I have ever witnessed is the 'dancing cranes' of Lake Hornborga in southern Sweden. They usually return from their Spanish wintering grounds in the last week of March, and by early April, when we visited, there were perhaps 10,000 cranes scattered around the grassy areas by the edge of the lake. During the winter they do not necessarily stay in pairs, so this is a crucial moment in these birds' lives. At this regular stopover point – they eventually nest further north – each bird needs to find its mate, and then perform an elaborate ritual to reaffirm their pair-bond.

How they do so, given that to the human eye all these birds look and sound identical, is something of a mystery. But their calls, which may be as distinctive to a crane as an individual human voice is to us, are a crucial element in the birds finding one another.

Once they are together, they then perform an extravagant and visually striking dance. One bird, usually the male, initiates the ritual by approaching his mate in a slow but stately walk, and then flapping his wings to attract her attention. As with other courtship rituals between birds, the female may choose to ignore him, indulging in what scientists call a 'displacement behaviour', such as feeding. But this is simply a test of his persistence; soon afterwards she will begin to respond, mirroring his movements while calling to him in a high-pitched sound, to which he in turn responds with a similar call and posture.

In full flow, when hundreds of cranes are dancing in synchrony, this is truly one of the world's greatest natural spectacles. And yet I have seen an even larger gathering of cranes, performing an even more remarkable display. This was in the Hula Valley, in Galilee in northern Israel, where we were filming an episode of the series *Birding with Bill Oddie*.

The weather had made it a tricky day, and when we arrived at the site, in late afternoon, a heavy downpour was in full swing. But as we were deciding whether to stay and film, or call it a day, the rain stopped, the clouds parted, and a rainbow appeared against the dark grey sky.

As if on cue, a flock of 20,000 cranes took off, swirled around in front of us, and finally drifted back down to land on the marsh. Then, lit up by the setting sun, pairs began to dance, jumping up into the air while uttering their haunting calls. I've been lucky enough to witness some pretty extraordinary natural events in my life, but this was without doubt the most memorable. For me, especially given their striking resemblance to human beings, it perfectly fits the image of the 'nine ladies dancing' of the Christmas carol.

Throughout much of the world, especially in Far Eastern cultures such as Japan and China, cranes are widely held to be sacred birds. Dances based on the cranes' rituals are regularly performed, while some specific styles of the martial art Kung Fu are inspired by the birds' postures and movements. In Asia, cranes are often seen, too, as symbols of eternal youth and happiness.

They are also linked with a poignant story of one of the victims of the atomic bomb that was dropped on the Japanese city of Hiroshima in August 1945.

At the time, Sadako Sasaki was just two years old; ten years later she was diagnosed with a deadly form of leukaemia, linked to the radiation produced by the explosion. While in hospital, the twelve-year-old was told of the ancient legend that anyone who can fold one thousand paper cranes, using the Japanese art of origami, will be granted their dearest wish. Sadako managed to complete the task, before dying in October of that year, and her legend lives on in Japanese culture, as one of the best known of the *hibakusha* – or 'bomb-affected persons'.

Other references to cranes go back to the earliest civilisations: the Greek poet Hesiod, writing around the seventh century BC, noted that the regular arrival of cranes each spring was a signal that ploughing should begin, while Homer, writing at roughly the same time as Hesiod, compared the cranes' far-carrying calls to the sound of an army going into battle.

Cranes also feature prominently in Aesop's *Fables*, with two appearances. In 'The Wolf and the Crane', a crane offers to take a bone out of the wolf's throat, and is then surprised when the wolf refuses to grant the promised reward; while 'The Geese and the Cranes' tells how, when a bird-catcher comes across a flock of birds feeding in the same field, the cranes manage to fly away, but the heavier, slower geese are caught.

The Roman writer Pliny told of how a crane will stand guard at night over the rest of his flock while they sleep, holding a stone in his claw so that, should he doze off, he will be woken by the noise of it falling. But in general, the Romans took a more utilitarian view of the birds, fattening them up in aviaries, after first blinding them.

Many writers have turned the cranes' epic journeys into poetry. In the fourteenth-century work *The Divine Comedy*, the Florentine poet Dante Alighieri made an early reference to the V-shaped formations they adopt to save energy while travelling:

> Chanting their dolorous notes, traverse the sky,
> Stretched out in long array . . .

More than a century later, another Florentine, Lorenzo de Medici – later known as 'Lorenzo the Magnificent' – was also entranced by the cranes' migratory journeys:

> Marking the tracts of air, the clamorous Cranes
> Wheel their due flight, in various lines descried;
> And each with out-stretched neck his rank maintains,
> In marshalled order through the ethereal void.

Admiration for these birds was not confined to Italian writers: in his epic seventeenth-century poem *Paradise Lost*, John Milton wrote of:

> Their airy caravan, high over seas
> Flying, and over lands, with mutual wing
> Easing their flight: so steers the prudent Crane
> Her annual voyage, borne on winds.

Modern writers have also been inspired by the movements of these birds, especially the sandhill and whooping cranes of North America. In her 1938 novel *The Yearling*, Marjorie Kinnan Rawlings wrote that:

Magic birds were dancing in the mystic marsh. The grass swayed with them, and the shallow waters, and the earth fluttered under them. The earth was dancing with the cranes, and the low sun, and the wind and sky.

In *A Sand County Almanac* her near-contemporary, the pioneering US environmentalist Aldo Leopold, also saw the cranes as having a meaning beyond their physical selves:

When we hear [the crane's] call we hear no mere bird. We hear the trumpet in the orchestra of evolution. He is the symbol of our untameable past, of that incredible sweep of millennia which underlies and conditions the daily affairs of birds and men.

Leopold's defence of the conservation importance of the crane came just in time for one of the world's rarest birds, the whooping crane. By 1938 the tallest bird in North America was on the very brink of extinction, with fewer than two dozen birds living in the wild. But thanks to last-ditch efforts the species was saved: today there are at least 800 whooping cranes alive – either in native or reintroduced populations in the wild, or in captivity, safeguarding the future of the species.

When they were still very rare, in 1975, the author and feminist Joanna Russ used them to make a valid political point about the lack of female representation in US politics, wryly noting that 'There are more whooping cranes in the United States of America than there are women in Congress.'

One of the greatest of all nature writers, the American Peter Matthiessen, spent his life documenting some of the most endangered creatures in the natural world, including the snow leopard, for which his eponymous book deservedly won many awards. Then, towards the end of his career, he went on a quest to see all the world's living species of crane, a journey that took him through five continents: North America, Europe, Africa, Asia and Australasia. The resulting book, *The Birds of Heaven* (published in 2001) explored the biological, ecological and cultural aspects of these birds' lives; indeed, for Matthiessen, as for many nature writers who have followed in his distinguished footsteps, the three categories are inextricably intertwined.

In his introduction to the book, Matthiessen tells of a dinner guest who, asking why he had been away from the delights of his Long Island home for the whole of the summer, was outraged when she discovered he had been in pursuit of cranes. 'Cranes?!' she squawked. 'Who cares about cranes?' Her response epitomised the level of ignorance amongst so many seemingly educated people when it comes to the importance of other species, and underscores the very point of the book.

As Matthiessen points out, in a message even more relevant today, when global water shortages are predicted to be one of the key issues of the coming century:

If one has truly understood a crane – or a leaf or a cloud or a frog – one has understood everything. In the growing scarcity of good water and the impending competition for this resource – which may become the greatest crisis for life on earth in the new millennium – the plight of *Homo* may not differ very much from that of *Grus*.

So what of the future of cranes, in Britain and around the world? Like other wetland species, they are an essential barometer for the health of our natural environment, so it is not surprising that several species – especially those in Asia – are suffering rapid and worrying declines.

Back home, though, this species represents hope. The reason cranes have not just survived but thrived here in Somerset, is down to the rewilding schemes that have created large areas of suitable wetland habitat for this and many other wetland species. Whereas a couple of decades ago only one species of long-legged waterbird, the familiar grey heron, could be found on the Somerset Levels, today up to a dozen species can be seen, including three different kinds of egret, three herons, two bitterns, glossy ibis, white stork, spoonbill and the crane. And of all these species, it is the crane that is the most special.

A couple of years ago, I was given a private guided tour of Sir Peter and Lady Philippa Scott's former home at Slimbridge. Looking out of the picture window, from where the world's most influential conservationist would draw and paint his beloved wildfowl, I was astonished to see a crane sitting on her nest on an island in the middle of the lake.

This was not, as I first assumed, from the captive bird collection, but one of those pioneering cranes that had been released in Somerset a few years earlier. Following some primal tracking instinct, she and her mate had found their way home to the very place where they had hatched, and decided to breed. What better symbol of hope for the future of our birds and wildlife?

Ten Lords A-Leaping

BLACK GROUSE

The scene reminded me of a nightclub in full swing. The lads were showing off, as only lads can do: shuffling back and forth in a manic dance, occasionally leaping high into the air, and shouting loudly to one another. All the while, they were pretending not to notice the lasses who had gathered around the edge of the dancefloor, patiently watching and waiting.

Sometimes the lads looked ready to fight, but their noisy bravado lacked the killer instinct. Only rarely did they come into contact with one another, let alone do any actual harm. Yet, despite appearances, it was clear that this was no game, but a deadly serious ritual. Only a few of the dozen or so males that were leaping around in front of me would get to mate with the females, and sire any offspring. The others, despite their finery and performance, hops and leaps, would die without issue.

Of course, this is not human behaviour I'm talking about: not even the most confident young man expects to win over every girl he meets. The display I was watching, from a cramped, chilly hide on a wild and windswept Scottish moor, was that of one of Britain's rarest and most compelling breeding birds: the black grouse.

Male black grouse – also known as 'blackcocks' – are one of a handful of birds around the world whose mating is performed at a lek. Deriving from the Swedish word *leka*, meaning 'to play', this is an all-or-nothing breeding strategy. The triumphant males – those that have leapt, danced and performed to the watching females' satisfaction – will end up mating with several females, while any males that do not come up to scratch will be left to themselves, and their sexual frustration.

Rather like the red deer rut, lekking involves great sacrifice on the part of the male birds: the long hours of performing use up valuable energy, and by displaying so prominently and loudly they make themselves very vulnerable to predators such as hawks and foxes. But although a huge gamble, for some it must be worth the effort, otherwise it would never have evolved as a breeding strategy.

Over the years, I have had the privilege of seeing many displays of birds, ranging from the spring dancing of great crested grebes to the winter murmuration of a million starlings. Yet that early April morning, when I spent a few hours in the company of a flock of lekking black grouse, easily takes the prize for the most incredible performance I have ever witnessed here in Britain. How could there be a better candidate for the 'ten lords a-leaping'?

The lek began just before dawn, which in April comes very early to these northern parts. To avoid disturbing the birds, I had to be inside the hide an hour or so before first light, which meant a very early start indeed. As I shivered, wishing I were back in my warm and cosy bed, I even momentarily wondered if all this effort would be worth it.

Then, out of the gloom, even before any songbirds had begun to herald the new day, I heard the first tentative sounds. Nothing prepares you for the call of a lekking male black grouse. It began as a soft, rather tuneful bubbling (known as 'rookooing'), interspersed with the occasional harsh, piercing screech, like a sheet of muslin being ripped in two. Once one started, the others soon joined in, until there was a cacophony of sound reaching my ears.

At first, I couldn't really make out the birds themselves: they were just dark, shadowy smudges against the background heather. But as my eyes gradually became accustomed to the scene, and the thin dawn light began to seep over the horizon, they finally came into sharp focus.

I could hardly believe what I was witnessing, as this spectacle unfolded on the grassy arena in front of the hide. Each male moved jerkily around, its wings spread, and head held down, as he manoeuvred for the prime position in the centre.

To complement their dancing skills, male black grouse have also evolved a complex and ornate plumage, making them one of the most striking and beautiful of all Britain's birds. These males did indeed appear black, at least at first but, as the light improved, I could begin to see shades of purple, deep brown and blue, topped by two red protuberances on the crown, all sharply contrasting with the snow-white, lyre-shaped tail held up behind each bird.

As the males moved up and down, occasionally leaping into the air as if overcome with pent-up sexual desire, they reminded me of a creature in an early computer-game, their jerky movements a result of the limitations of technology. The sound, too, had an animatronic quality, as if a dove's cooing had been fed through a synthesiser, then played at full volume through distorted speakers. All in all, it was a rather disorienting experience: in many ways, these birds were some of the least birdlike I had ever seen, and yet they were also amongst the most beautiful.

After a while, I noticed a female sitting unobtrusively at the edge of the lekking arena, concealed in the heather. Female black grouse are known as 'greyhens', on account of their speckled, brownish-grey plumage. They may look as if they are powerless, in the face of all this masculine posturing, yet the very opposite is the case. Females are powerful because *they* do the choosing: only once the males have performed, and retired exhausted from the fray, do the greyhens indicate which ones they are prepared to mate with.

That brief sexual encounter marks the end of the male's involvement in the relationship. He will take no further part in incubating the clutch of up to eleven eggs, feeding the female or raising the chicks; indeed, he may well never even see his offspring. His only duty is to provide the sperm to fertilise the female. He has that in common with all lekking birds, including the ruff, and his larger cousin the capercaillie.

That the black grouse is able to have such a bizarre breeding strategy is all down to diet. The food their chicks need – small insects such as caterpillars and the larvae of flies – is found throughout their woodland and moorland habitat; while that

required by the adults – mainly heather shoots, birch catkins and berries – is also widely available.

This means that, unlike most other birds, the males have no need to hold and defend a territory. Instead, they can indulge in their unusual breeding strategy to their heart's content, while the poor females do all the work. As the Victorian conservationist W. H. Hudson wrote:

At the end of winter many birds meet together at an early hour of the morning, when the males utter their powerful call-notes, and strut to and fro, with tail expanded and trailing wings, in the presence of the hens. These 'matrimonial markets' are scenes of desperate combats between rival cocks. In the end each male retires with the females he has secured for his harem.

Thomas Bewick, writing a century earlier, was even more taken with the performance of the males, and in particular the aftermath of victory, in which the winning male postures like a champion prize-fighter:

> On the return of spring the males assemble in great numbers at their accustomed resorts . . . when the contest for superiority commences, and continues with great bitterness until the vanquished are put to flight: the victors being left in possession of the field, place themselves on an eminence, clap their wings, and with loud cries give notice to their females, who immediately resort to the spot.

Although they look much larger when lekking, because they puff out their feathers to look more impressive, black grouse are actually about the same size as a pheasant, though much stockier. Males are about 53 cm (21 inches) long, and weigh in at between 1 and 1.4 kg (2.2–3.1 lbs). The females are about a quarter smaller and lighter.

The British Isles are at the very westernmost edge of the black grouse's range, which stretches right across the forested mid-latitudes of Europe and Asia, all the way to eastern China. It has one closely-related 'sister species', the Caucasian black grouse which, as its name suggests, is confined to the Caucasus mountain range of south-eastern Europe.

Like many other species of the boreal forests, the black grouse prefers to live on the edge of the wooded habitat known as 'forest-steppe', where the trees thin out into moorland, and the ground becomes boggier. The mixture of wooded and more open habitats enables the birds to find food such as heather and various kinds of berry in summer and twigs, buds and catkins in winter. Although these areas often appear 'natural', they are usually the result of traditional farming, with grazing animals helping to keep the forest more open, and so creating a mix of different 'mini-habitats'.

With an estimated world population of between fifteen and forty million birds, the black grouse is not considered to be globally endangered, though, as with many species that require a variety of habitats, it is suffering local declines, especially in the more developed, western parts of its range.

Along with so many other widespread north European species, the black grouse was first described and named by the 'father of taxonomy', the Swede Carl Linnaeus, in 1758. He gave it the scientific name *Tetrao tetrix*, which it still bears. Yet the species was known in Britain from well before then: 'In all the Moore-land and Mosse-land of Scotland', wrote John Monipennie in 1603 in one of the earliest printed books, 'doth resort the blacke Cocke, a fowle of a marueilous beautie.' At that time the species was not only found throughout Scotland, but was also resident in every English county.

Yet by the time 'The Twelve Days of Christmas' first appeared in English, around 1780, the black grouse was already, it seems, in decline: the Reverend Gilbert White, whose bestselling book

The Natural History of Selborne was published in 1789, lamented the species' disappearance from the area around his Hampshire home, which had occurred during his own lifetime:

> There was a nobler species of game in this forest, now extinct, which I have heard old people say abounded much . . . and that was the *heath-cock*, *black game*, or *grouse*. When I was a little boy [in the 1720s] I recollect one coming now and then to my father's table. The last pack I remember was killed about thirty-five years ago; and within these ten years one solitary *grey hen* was sprung by some beagles in beating for a hare. The sportsmen cried out, 'A hen pheasant', but a gentleman present, who had often seen grouse in the north of England, assured me that it was a grey hen.

Like its cousin the red grouse, the black grouse was considered great 'sport', because of its wariness and fast, low flight. In 1884, a correspondent to the *Pall Mall Gazette* lamented his inability to bag one: 'As for blackcock, the wary old birds sail in the open over the moor a hundred yards out of shot.' But with skill and persistence they did fall to the guns, as the early nineteenth century sportsman and portrait-painter, William Smellie Watson, boasted:

> In the course of two hours . . . we bagged thirty birds, and had we not been interrupted by a very heavy thunder shower, we should have doubled that number.

Being large and plump, they also made good eating. 'I would-na say just what's intil the pie,' reflects a character in John Buchan's 1927 novel *Witch Wood*, 'but at any rate there's black-cocks and snipes and leverets, for I had the shooting of them.'

During Queen Victoria's reign, the steady decline of the species continued. This was mainly due to the rising popularity of hunting, which from the middle of the nineteenth century had become far more efficient, through the increased use of the breech-loading shotgun. The onset of enclosure, which replaced the traditional strip-farming landscape with the 'patchwork-quilt' countryside we know today, also had a negative effect, as it vastly reduced the amount of open 'wastes' on which the black grouse thrived. This inevitably led to a fall in numbers.

The species' range began to steadily retreat to the north and west, and it still bred in the wilder and less densely populated areas of mid-Wales, northern England and Scotland, where suitable habitat remained. Shooting, ironically, briefly gave the black grouse a helping hand, with birds being artificially reintroduced to several sites, including the royal estate at Sandringham in Norfolk, from where they later spread to neighbouring areas.

Yet as early as 1861, the ornithologist and author J. C. Atkinson lamented that 'the gradual and very complete demolition of the last remains of what were once very extensive forests has completely banished the Black Grouse from places where it used to be very common within the memory of living men.'

By the 1880s, a century after Gilbert White, the black grouse had almost entirely disappeared from south-east England, although it managed to survive on the higher ground of Exmoor and Dartmoor in the south-west, with smaller numbers on the heathlands of Dorset and the New Forest. These moors and heaths provided exactly what the species needed: plenty of food, forested habitats, and more open, grassy areas where they could find an arena for performing their displays.

But the black grouse's range continued to shrink throughout the twentieth century, so that, having bred in almost sixty counties in the period from 1875 to 1900, by the time of the first BTO *Atlas* survey, which took place from 1968 to 1972, they could only be found in forty.

From then on, the decline accelerated. Today, the black grouse is mostly confined to Scotland and the central belt of northern England, with small, outlying populations in North Wales and the North Midlands. Back in 1869, in *The Birds of Somersetshire*, Cecil Smith could still write that 'The grand old "Black Cock" is still, and I hope will long continue, tolerably plentiful in such parts of the county that are suited to its habits.' Sadly, the species has long since disappeared from my home county. The very last bird, a greyhen, was recorded at Chetsford Water on Exmoor on 29 July 1981, poignantly silhouetted against a beacon lit on Dunkery to commemorate the wedding of Prince Charles and Lady Diana Spencer.

As with so many birds, including the turtle dove and grey partridge, the decline of the black grouse is largely down to habitat change and loss. Modern farming and forestry methods simply do not work for this species, which needs a complex mosaic of habitats where the females can find enough food to single-handedly raise a family each spring.

However, the recent decline may also have been hastened by another factor: climate change. A series of cool, wet Junes has had a very negative effect on new-born chicks, which struggle to survive as they follow their mother through the dense, wet vegetation.

The black grouse remains a common occurrence at least in our culture, especially in Scotland. Their tails – with their bright white feathers – were used in Victorian times to adorn hats (known as 'Tam o'Shanters') worn with traditional Highland dress. Even today, they are sported by members of pipe bands, as well as various Scottish regiments.

More gruesomely, on the Hebridean isle of Lewis, the blood of a blackcock was used to treat shingles, while the devil is reputed to appear in the shape of a black dog or black cock – though this could, of course, be referring to a cockerel rather than a grouse. Yet the call of the black grouse was also seen as a positive omen: as Victorian ornithologist William MacGillivray noted, 'By its crowing at dawn the evil spirits of night are put to flight or deprived of their power.'

MacGillivray, a Scot who would have observed lekking black grouse on many occasions, was a great admirer of the species, which he described as 'one of the most beautiful, and in several respects one of the most remarkable, of all our native birds'. He also noted several examples of hybrid pairings between the black grouse and the pheasant, rather than, as we might expect, its closer relatives the ptarmigan and red grouse. These may have occurred, MacGillivray suggested, because of the solitary nature of the greyhens, which might lead them to hybridise more freely than the other species of grouse, which form pairs in which the male will defend his territory and his mate against intruders from his or any other species.

Our fascination with this captivating gamebird continues to this day. The 'Famous Grouse' brand of whisky, whose label shows an image of a red grouse, is mass-produced for everyday drinking. But for the dedicated whisky connoisseur, the company also produces a more expensive, limited-edition brand, with a more sophisticated, smoky flavour than the standard variety. Naturally, this is called 'The Black Grouse'.

Sadly, as the black grouse's decline continues, with only about 5,000 males remaining in the whole of Britain, it is getting harder and harder to witness these magnificent 'lords a-leaping'. The last time I did so was one February morning in a hidden corner of Speyside in the Scottish Highlands. It was the last day of our family holiday, and it took a lot of persuasion to get my children up so early. But once everything was packed and ready for the long journey south it was well worth it: even from a distance, parked in a layby on a public road, we enjoyed great views of the lek.

Then, just as we were about to leave, a huge bird-of-prey swept down from the surrounding trees, and scattered the males, which flew straight over our heads as though in formation for a flying display. The predator was a goshawk, and although on that occasion it was unsuccessful, it reminded me just how exposed these birds are as they perform the role of a lifetime.

Eleven Pipers Piping

SANDPIPERS

A fine day in late April, along the banks of the River Spey, home to the bird I think of as the inspiration for the 'eleven pipers piping'. At this time of year, the river begins to come alive after the rigours of the long, hard winter that saw a layer of ice formed over the surface and snow blanketing the banks.

The start of spring signals a rush of activity for the various birds that breed by these fast-flowing waters, rich in the tiny aquatic insects they feed their young. Many of these species are resident, found here or hereabouts all the year round. But one little wader has just arrived, having spent the last few months in sub-Saharan Africa. It lands on one of the water-splashed rocks in the middle of the white-foamed river, bobs up and down, and then flies off downstream on rapidly whirring wings.

On its way it utters a high-pitched, piping call: three piercing notes that cut through the constant sonic backdrop of rushing waters. The combination of the call, the riverine habitat, the drone-like flight action and the dapper appearance of the bird itself, means it can only be a common sandpiper.

I don't much like that word 'common' in the name of a bird: for me it demeans what often turns out to be a fascinating species. That's definitely the case for the common sandpiper, one of the most attractive and endearing of all our small waders.

Such a familiar bird was bound to come to the attention of Gilbert White, though he noted that it was 'said to belong to the north only'. This reflects the common sandpiper's preference for fast-flowing rivers and streams, which are indeed mostly in the higher northern and western parts of Britain. However, White also recalled that a cock bird 'haunted the banks of some ponds near the village; and as it had a companion, doubtless meant to have bred near that water'.

In Thomas Bewick's two-volume guide *A History of British Birds*, published at the turn of the nineteenth century, he included a splendidly concise description: '[They] are well known by their clear piping note, by their flight, by jerking up their tails, and by their manner of running after their insect prey on the pebbly margins of brooks and rivers.'

Common sandpipers feed on a wide range of insects and other invertebrates, including flies and their larvae, beetles, spiders, freshwater shrimps and occasionally small fish. The most frequent feeding method is to perch, walk or, as Bewick noted, run along close to the water, and pick their tiny prey off the surface, using their straight, pointed bill. When feeding, common sandpipers often bob up and down in a regular motion. They are not the only riparian bird to do this: two other species often found in the same habitat, the grey wagtail and the dipper, are also known for this repetitive bobbing. Indeed, the dipper earned its name from this characteristic behaviour.

There are no fewer than three different theories for why these river birds do this. The most widely accepted is that moving rapidly up and down breaks up the bird's outline, thus helping to conceal it from watching predators. Another suggestion is that as the bird bobs, it is better able to see through the reflections on the surface of the water, and so spot its prey.

But there are problems with both of these explanations: first, the fact that other birds, which hunt on land, do not show this behaviour; and secondly, that by moving so obviously the bird surely draws attention to its presence, rather than concealing it.

For me, the most plausible solution to the mystery is that in this noisy environment, bobbing or dipping up and down enables the bird to communicate with its mate or chicks nearby. This is also why all these species have such a high-pitched call: higher-frequency notes cut through the background noise of the river much better than lower.

Common sandpipers have also evolved an unusual strategy to escape from predators, noted by the nineteenth-century ornithologist William Yarrell. He told of a sandpiper that, when pursued across a river by a hawk, plunged beneath the water to escape, and waited until the predator had flown away, before emerging unharmed.

A few decades later, W. H. Hudson confirmed this observation, noting that 'both old and young birds are able to swim with ease, and, to escape danger, dive as readily as a moorhen or water-rail.' A rather odd observation, since neither of those two species regularly dive – perhaps he was thinking of the coot or little grebe.

The common sandpiper is, when seen well, very easy to

identify: a small-to-medium-sized wader, a fraction smaller and lighter than a song thrush, though with much longer legs and bill. It is dark olive-brown above, and white below, with a dark head, neck and breast, greenish legs, and a narrow white stripe through and around the eye, giving the bird a rather quizzical appearance. In flight, the bird reveals thin white wingbars.

This is a fairly common breeding species in Britain, with roughly 15,000 pairs, though, as White pointed out, it is found mainly in the uplands of the north and west. But this may not always have been the case. During the nineteenth century, the species appears to have been equally at home on lowland rivers and streams, and indeed in Ireland it preferred to nest at lower, rather than higher, elevations.

It is something of a mystery as to exactly when the common sandpiper began to decline as a breeding bird in lowland Britain. It started to disappear from Devon and Cornwall during the first half of the twentieth century, although a few pairs do still breed along the river Dart in South Devon.

The good news for those of us in the south is that on migration – any time from March to April in spring, and July to September in autumn – common sandpipers can be seen alongside many different waterbodies, from inland gravel pits, rivers and streams to pools near the coast. I regularly come across them on my coastal patch in Somerset, where they reveal their presence by flitting low over the muddy waters of the Brue estuary, uttering that distinctive call.

Not all the birds I see here are our own breeding birds: many hail from Scandinavia, and are simply passing through on their way to and from their winter-quarters in Spain or Morocco. British breeding birds usually head further south, to West Africa, though each year a handful of them do stay put for the winter.

Elsewhere, common sandpipers breed across a broad swathe of Europe and Asia, all the way from Ireland and Iberia in the west to Kamchatka and Japan in the east, and from beyond the Arctic Circle in the north to Iran in the south. Eastern populations winter from the Middle East, via India, to Australia, while western birds head to Africa. On visits to Kenya and Tanzania I have often come across common sandpipers bobbing up and down in the incongruous setting of a waterhole, surrounded by elephants, zebras and other exotic animals.

Worldwide, there are two dozen different species with 'sandpiper' in their name, which in turn are part of a much larger family of waders, including curlews, godwits, shanks, woodcocks and snipes.

The sandpipers are mostly globetrotting birds, known for their epic, long-distance migrations, and can be found in every continent apart from Antarctica. They include familiar species such as the green and wood sandpipers in the Old World, and pectoral and white-rumped sandpipers in the New, as well as some very rare species such as the Tuamotu sandpiper, found only on the South Pacific island of that name, in French Polynesia. But the little bird hunting assiduously for food along a Scottish river is the true original.

According to John Ray and Francis Willughby, whose pioneering *Ornithology* was published in 1678, 'sandpiper' was originally a Yorkshire word for the species. Several commentators have described the name as 'self-explanatory', confirmed by the species' genus, *Actitis*, which means 'coast-dweller'. Yet of all our wading birds, common sandpipers are one of the least likely to be seen on sandy beaches, even during migration. Perhaps the name was originally applied to a beach-haunting wader, such as the dunlin or sanderling, and only later transferred to this species.

There are also a host of folk-names for the common sandpiper, many of which originate in Scotland, where the bird is still

common and widespread. They fall into three main categories: deriving either from the bird's sound, its preferred habitat, or its habits.

The first group, which comes from that piercing call, includes 'heather peeper', 'waterypleeps', 'dickie-di-dee', 'willy wicket' and simply 'weet weet'. The redoubtable William MacGillivray, an eccentric Scotsmen who attempted – and spectacularly failed – to persuade his fellow Victorians that they should standardise the English names of birds, proposed renaming this species 'The White-breasted Weet-weet', which certainly does what it says on the tin.

The second category of folk-names – those from the sandpiper's (supposed) habitat – include 'sand lark', 'sandie laverock' (laverock being an old name for lark), 'sand snipe' and 'shore snipe'.

The comparison with the much longer-billed snipe also surfaces in the third category: names that derive from the bird's habits or time of its arrival, such as 'summer snipe'. MacGillivray also reported the Hebridean name 'little fiddler', which he described as coming 'from the manner in which this bird continually vibrates its body, as if on a pivot, joined with its piping notes'. It's a lovely image.

The most baffling of these names is, at least on the surface, 'shad bird', which refers to the common freshwater fish, a member of the herring family. According to the Revd Charles Swainson, whose 1885 work *The Folk Lore and Provincial Names of British Birds* is a comprehensive collection of now mostly defunct folknames, the unusual name links the bird with a seasonal movement of the fish:

Before the erection of weirs at Worcester and other places on the Severn, shad used to ascend the river; they came up about the middle of April, at the time of the arrival of the common sandpiper; and it is probable that the Severn fishermen, connecting the appearance of the bird with the advent of the shad-fishing season, gave to it the local appellation of shad-bird.

Whether on the River Severn or elsewhere, common sandpipers are not, sadly, as common as they used to be. The acidification of rivers has reduced the availability of the insects on which they feed, while the constant disturbance from anglers, walkers, boats and other river users can also affect their chances of raising a family.

Of the other twenty-three sandpiper species, four are either rare breeders, passage migrants or winter visitors to Britain, while another fifteen are vagrants or occasional visitors, mostly from North America.

In winter and on passage, green and wood sandpipers are birds of freshwater wetlands; but in spring and summer they breed in the vast boreal forests, or taiga, of northern Eurasia. Apart from the oceans, this is the largest biome (distinctive community of plants and animals) in the world. This huge, mostly coniferous forest stretches right across the northern part of North America, and in Eurasia from Scandinavia and Scotland in the west, to the Japanese island of Hokkaido in the east. From south to north it occurs from roughly 50 degrees to 70 degrees north, just inside the Arctic Circle.

Both green and wood sandpipers pass through Britain – mainly in early autumn – and regularly turn up on my home patch, the Avalon Marshes in Somerset, especially on the pools left behind after peat has been removed. On a hot day in late July, when autumn is the last thing on my mind, I may hear a powerful, piping, three-note whistle. Louder and more strident than the call of the common sandpiper, this announces that the first autumn migrant, a green sandpiper, has arrived. Usually the sound is accompanied by a flash of black and white, as what appears to be a giant house martin streaks low away across the surface of the water. In the process it shows off its pure-white rump, before momentarily rising up into the air, and then plummeting down into a new hiding place in the reeds.

If I am lucky enough to see a green sandpiper on the ground – and this doesn't happen very often – the contrast between the dark green upperparts and bright white underparts is very distinctive; it is also noticeably larger than the common sandpiper.

On my return home, I may casually mention to my wife Suzanne that autumn has begun, which guarantees an unsympathetic response, with the suggestion that I am wishing the summer away. But in all seriousness, the first green sandpiper – which I have recorded as early as 14 July – is indeed such a sign, for although one or two pairs do breed each year at secret sites in the Scottish Highlands, virtually all those we see in Britain come from further north.

By late September, the vast majority of green sandpipers have already passed through Britain and are several thousand miles to the south, in north-west Africa. But small numbers – perhaps a hundred or so – choose to stay put in Britain, spending the winter in narrow ditches and dykes, where few other birds choose to venture. One December, Suzanne was walking our Labrador around the moor at the back of our house when a slender wading bird flew up from the muddy bottom of a rhyne (the local name for a water-filled ditch), and zig-zagged away in haste, making a piping call. Even without binoculars, she suspected it was a green sandpiper, and she was right.

Given that it is such an easily-overlooked bird, the green sandpiper has still managed to accumulate a handful of folk-names. Some, such as 'martin snipe' and 'black sandpiper', relate to its appearance, while 'drain snipe' is a clear reference to its habitat. But my favourite is 'whistling sandpiper', a tribute to its distinctive piping call.

The wood sandpiper, whose understated elegance makes it for me one of the most attractive members of its family, is a far scarcer visitor to Somerset, and indeed to Britain as a whole; for this reason, it has never acquired an English folk-name. Yet about a dozen pairs breed here each year, in the remotest parts of the Scottish Highlands and neighbouring Flow Country. In autumn, they can turn up almost anywhere, though they are more regular along the east coast of Britain.

Normally, wood sandpipers are fairly scarce in spring, but one May, a few years ago, a pair chose to spend a few days on Tealham Moor, an area of wet, boggy meadows just down the road from my home. Seeing them in their spanking-new breeding plumage, with their sparkling buff-on-brown upperparts, bright yellow legs and slender physique, was a real treat. Alas, they soon departed north.

I've seen wood and green sandpipers in many other parts of the world, as, like their smaller cousin, these are truly global travellers. Indeed, on the very first morning of my first ever birding trip abroad, to Northern India in February 1985, I rose early to take a walk outside our hotel near Delhi Airport. To my surprise and delight, on a muddy pool on a piece of waste ground I found both wood and green sandpipers feeding alongside their rarer cousin, the marsh sandpiper. Many years later, in Tanzania, I watched both species feeding on mud alongside several large crocodiles, seemingly unafraid of these huge reptiles, who looked as if they could finish off a sandpiper with the same thoughtless ease we would bring to eating a crisp.

But my most memorable encounter of all took place in a forest in eastern Poland, back in the late 1990s. I heard a bird singing from the top of a larch: a sound completely unfamiliar to me, although something about its tone reminded me of a thrush. Then my friend and guide Marek Borkowski came alongside, and announced that it was a green sandpiper. What I had naturally assumed to be a songbird was a wader, singing from a perch near its nest, which it had in turn taken over from another species, probably a fieldfare.

Neither of the other two sandpipers regularly seen in Britain breeds here, unless you count the very occasional nesting attempt by purple sandpipers, again in the Scottish Highlands. This is normally a bird found on rocky coasts, usually in the

Tail of the Common Sandpiper
(*Actitis hypoleucos*).

company of another Arctic breeding wader, the turnstone.

Even though as many as 13,000 purple sandpipers spend the winter around our coasts, they can be easy to miss. Their name may suggest a panoply of mauve and violet, lilac or lavender, but the truth is rather more mundane. Outside the breeding season, purple sandpipers are mainly dark grey in colour, relieved only by their yellowish legs and the distinctive yellow base of their short, stubby bill. Like turnstones, they feed on a range of tidal crustaceans and gastropods, including winkles, crabs and shrimps.

This is a bird for whom the word 'diffident' might have been invented. They sit tightly on rocks, usually in small flocks, so it is very easy to overlook them, especially at high tide. From the same genus as the dunlin and knot – and so only distantly related to the common, green and wood sandpipers – they are one of the most overlooked of all regularly occurring British birds. Even their Shetland folk-name, 'stanepecker' (stone pecker) is rather dull.

In spring, though, purple sandpipers undergo a change in appearance, as their head and back take on a purplish hue. It may not be especially dramatic, but it does explain how the species got its name. One memorable May morning, many years ago, I saw them like this: not on their Scandinavian breeding grounds but closer to home, on the Hebridean island of South Uist, where a flock had stopped off to feed along the sandy shore on their way north.

But when usually seen, on a bleak winter's day, the purple sandpiper's rather dark, stumpy appearance, and its habit of sleeping for long periods of time on slippery, seaweed-covered rocks, make it rather unexciting. Yet we should not underestimate them: as the nature-writer Ian Parsons puts it, this is a bird that 'really does live on the edge, existing in the ever-changing border between sea and land'.

The remaining British sandpiper is in the same genus, but a more attractive bird, with a more appropriate name. The curlew sandpiper takes its name from its much larger relative the curlew, as it also sports a long, de-curved bill.

By rights, this species should not be a regular visitor to Britain at all, as their nearest breeding grounds are a quarter of the way around the world, on the Arctic tundra stretching eastwards from the remote Yenisei Delta in Siberia. The breeding range is very small, especially compared to where they can be found during the rest of the year: curlew sandpipers spend the winter in the Rift Valley, India and Australia, western and southern Africa, travelling up to 15,000 km (9,300 miles) each way.

Species that also nest alongside the curlew sandpiper, such as Terek and broad-billed sandpipers, are rare vagrants to Britain, as when they have finished breeding they head south and east. But, unusually, curlew sandpipers instead travel westwards, and so pass through Britain from August onwards on their long loop to West Africa.

Like many waders, the juvenile birds, hatched earlier in the year, migrate first, sporting their clean, fresh feathers in various shades of pale buff and brown. Later, from September onwards, they are followed by their parents, some of which may be in almost full breeding plumage, with dashing and rather gaudy brick-red underparts.

Because the curlew sandpiper has the smallest breeding range, compared with its non-breeding range, of any shorebird, it is very vulnerable to environmental change. Numbers on its wintering grounds have fallen by almost half in the past forty years or so, making the species a serious cause for conservation concern.

You might think that the final clutch of 'pipers piping' – the appropriate total of eleven assorted New World sandpipers – have no place in a book on a British Christmas tradition, or indeed on British birds at all. Yet in autumn, the tail-end of hurricanes and autumn gales, aided by the powerful North Atlantic Jetstream, does bring these birds to our shores.

They are, in roughly descending order of regularity of appearance: pectoral, buff-breasted, spotted, white-rumped, Baird's, upland, solitary, stilt, semipalmated, western and least sandpipers. The last of these is the smallest of the world's 200 or so species of wader: as little as 13 cm (5 inches) long and weighing a mere 20 grams (two-thirds of an ounce), making it even smaller than a sparrow.

Many of these globetrotting waders turn up in good numbers and at regular sites every autumn: the commonest, the pectoral sandpiper (named after its distinctive breast-band), averages more than 50 records a year. Its regular arrival here raises several important questions: first, given their regularity, can pectoral sandpipers be considered 'vagrants' at all? And is there not a chance that one day at least one of these American sandpipers will colonise Britain and Europe as a breeding bird?

In fact, there is only one breeding record of any North American sandpiper in Britain: a pair of spotted sandpipers – the polka-dot cousin of our common sandpiper – which were discovered nesting along the banks of a Highland river in June 1975. This pioneering duo laid four eggs, but sadly failed to raise any young – the nest was either trampled by cattle or flattened by heavy rain. But perhaps, as weather patterns change and autumnal gales grow fiercer and more frequent, one of these Yankee waders will eventually manage to colonise the Old World.

Twelve Drummers Drumming

WOODPECKERS

When we hear the final line of this carol, the image that first comes to mind might be that of an Irish pipe band, with young men twirling drumsticks, or perhaps the Royal Scots Guards, with busby-clad guardsmen thumping loudly on their big bass drums. In the world of birds, though, there are two main avian contenders for the last line, 'Twelve drummers drumming'. Oddly, they both make their sound using non-vocal means, which is rather unusual in the avian world.

The first candidate is the common snipe, which on spring and summer evenings rises high into the sky over the wet meadows where it breeds, and then swoops up and down through the warm air like a stunt pilot doing power dives. I have stood on the flower-strewn Hebridean *machair*, my feet soaked in dew, and listened to this strange sound, to my ears more bubbling than percussive, known as 'drumming'.

It was long assumed, naturally, that this sound was made vocally, though William Yarrell suggested a more directly physical source:

> The male bird . . . [makes] a humming or bleating noise, not un-
> like that of a goat, apparently produced by a peculiar action of
> the wings, as the bird, whenever the sound is emitted, is observed
> to descend with great velocity, and with a trembling motion of
> the pinions.

Yarrell's speculation was not that far off the mark. Yet it took another century before the mystery of the snipe's peculiar drumming display was solved, by the zoologist and physician Sir Philip Manson-Bahr. He deduced that the sound was produced not by the bird's voice, or by the wings, as Yarrell and many other observers had thought, but by using its tail. When the snipe rises into the air, it spreads its specially adapted tail-feathers like a fan, holding the two outermost feathers out at a 90-degree angle. As the bird speeds down to the Earth like a kamikaze pilot, the rapidly-moving air vibrates through them, producing that incredible drumming sound.

Clearly a man with a theatrical bent, Manson-Bahr decided to reveal the solution at a dinner of the members and fellows of that august and serious body the British Ornithologists' Union, held at a rather sleazy Italian restaurant in London's Soho. He did so by inserting two of the snipe's tail-feathers into a cork, which he then spun around his head on a string to re-create the drumming sound, thus conclusively proving his point.

But strong though the snipe's association with drumming may be, the birds we associate the word with more than any other family are, of course, the woodpeckers. Go into an ancient woodland on a bright, calm morning in late winter or early spring, and the chances are you will soon hear a rapid burst of sound, lasting two or three seconds, rather like someone drumming their fingers incredibly rapidly on a hollow piece of wood.

If you manage to catch a glimpse of the bird, it will almost certainly be a great spotted woodpecker: about the size of a blackbird, with a distinctive black-and-white plumage (hence the old name of 'pied woodpecker'). It may also have a red patch on its belly, just above the tail, and a red blob on the back of its head, denoting that this is a male.

This woodpecker is doing exactly what all the songbirds in the wood are doing at this time of year: 'singing' to defend his territory and attract a mate. But instead of using his syrinx (the bird equivalent of our larynx and vocal cords), he moves his head rapidly back and forward like a sewing machine, banging the tip of his beak against a dead branch or trunk of a tree up to sixteen times per second to create this unique sound.

Although drumming is primarily done by the male, for territorial purposes, female woodpeckers may also drum, perhaps to sound the alarm at approaching danger, or simply to communicate with one another in their densely wooded home.

The key to successful drumming is resonance: the sound needs to carry through the air to reach rival males and interested females. So the male will usually take time to choose a particular dead branch, with a hollow centre, which helps him create that echoing sound. In Britain, and elsewhere around the world, woodpeckers have been known to drum on man-made objects, such as telegraph poles, fence posts, chimneys and the sides of houses. In one celebrated incident involving a group of yellow-shafted flickers (a medium-sized North American species of woodpecker), the birds managed to delay the launch of the Space Shuttle at Florida's Cape Canaveral, by pecking holes in its outer surface.

Drumming woodpeckers have evolved several unique anatomical features, to allow them to perform without either falling off the tree or causing physical damage to themselves. They have thicker skulls than other similar-sized birds, with sponge-like padding to dampen the impact of repeatedly banging their head against what must feel like a brick wall. Their neck muscles are also stronger than normal, and their short, sharp and powerful bill is surrounded by rictal bristles, which stop particles of wood from damaging their eyesight. Like owls, cuckoos and swifts, woodpeckers also have zygodactyl feet, with two toes facing forward and two facing back: this helps them grip the bark of trees when ascending them.

Watch a woodpecker either when it is drumming or when it is simply climbing up the trunk of a tree, and you'll also notice it uses its tail to brace itself – again, the tail feathers are stiffer than those of other birds. This was something noted by Thomas Bewick, author and illustrator of the first prototype 'field guide' to British birds, who remarked on the tail's 'stiff, sharp, pointed feathers, rough on the undersides and bent inwards, by which it supports itself on the trunks of trees while in search of food'. Bewick was clearly taken by woodpeckers as a family:

> Their characters are striking, and their manners singular. The bill
> is large, strong, and fitted for its employment: the end of it is

sharp and formed like a wedge, with which it pierces the bark of trees, and bores through the wood in which its food is lodged.

He went on to note that the sound a drumming woodpecker makes is 'by a succession of strokes repeated with surprising rapidity', long before this was finally confirmed by the use of slow-motion film. He also realised, no doubt by close examination of museum specimens, another unique characteristic of the family: the long, curved tongue, with 'a curious muscular apparatus . . . spirally arranged on the sides of its head, almost encircling each eye'.

Woodpeckers are as diverse as virtually any family of birds. There are more than 200 different species, found in every continent apart from Australasia and Antarctica, living everywhere from north of the Arctic Circle to the storm-swept island of Tierra del Fuego in the south.

The smallest species, the minuscule bar-breasted piculet of South America, is just three inches (7.5 cm) long, and weighs a mere third of an ounce (roughly 8–10 grams) – about the same as a wren. The largest, the aptly-named imperial woodpecker of the Sierra Madre mountains in Mexico, was up to 24 inches (60 cm) long. I say 'was' because, tragically, this impressive black, white and red-crested woodpecker is now almost certainly extinct, as a result of a campaign by foresters during the 1950s, who placed poison on trees where the birds foraged, and wiped out a thriving population in just a few years.

Britain has a mere four species of woodpecker: green, great spotted, lesser spotted and the wryneck, which looks very different from other woodpeckers, and does not drum. Although once common and familiar throughout southern Britain, the wryneck is now more or less extinct as a British breeding bird, though pairs do occasionally nest in the Scottish Highlands. Today, if you see one at all, it is when Scandinavian birds pass along our east coast, mainly in autumn.

Cross the English Channel, and you will find eleven different species of woodpecker, whose main strongholds are in the extensive ancient forests of eastern Europe and Scandinavia. The reason for the paucity of species in Britain relates to woodpeckers' limited powers of flight: they are either unable, or extremely reluctant, to cross large areas of water. So when, 8,000 years or so ago, a rise in sea levels separated us from the rest of Europe, only those four species had managed to make it on to our shores following their retreat during the previous Ice Age. Ireland fared even less well: no woodpecker species made it there at all. However, in the past decade or so, the great spotted woodpecker has finally managed to cross the Irish Sea and establish itself on the Emerald Isle.

Woodpeckers do fly, of course, though generally only for short distances. Even in silhouette, they are easy to pick out, as Gilbert White noticed: 'Woodpeckers fly *volatu undoso*, opening and closing their wings at every stroke, and so are always rising or falling in curves.'

That undulating flight, with deep wingbeats interspersed with short glides, is often marked by the loud, metallic *'chip'* call of the great spotted, or the laughing sound of the green woodpecker. Very different from other similar-sized birds, the flight action provides an easy way to spot them as they bounce from one place to another.

The green woodpecker is our largest species, about the size of a pigeon, and the second largest in Europe (after the crow-sized black woodpecker). As its name suggests, the green woodpecker is predominantly yellowish-green, darker above than below, with a black 'highwayman's mask' around its staring yellow eyes, and a red crown and nape. In flight, it often shows its bright yellow rump as it heads rapidly away from you.

Unlike its spotted cousins, the green woodpecker is usually seen on the ground, where it forages for ants, using that huge, coiled tongue to vacuum them up in their hundreds. As Bewick noted, this species:

> is seen more frequently on the ground than the other kinds, particularly where there are ant-hills. It inserts its long tongue into the holes through which the ants issue, and draws out those insects in abundance.

Sometimes I've managed to get surprisingly close to a feeding green woodpecker before it noticed me. But my closest encounter of all was when my daughter Daisy (then aged about eight) inadvertently flushed one into our greenhouse. I rescued the frightened bird, which stared at us with a cold, unblinking eye. It also stuck its tongue out until it was longer than its bill: a memorable sight.

Both green and great spotted woodpeckers are doing rather well, countering the declining trend of many woodland birds. That is partly because, like species such as the blackbird and blue tit, they have adapted well to living alongside us in parks and gardens, even in the heart of towns and cities. Great spotted woodpeckers, in particular, have found a bounteous supply of food in our suburban gardens, in the form of baby birds taken from nests and even nestboxes, which they can bore into using that powerful bill. Yet although they probably take as many baby birds as that other notorious black-and-white nest predator, the magpie, they mostly do so out of sight, and so have escaped being demonised in the tabloid press.

Both the larger woodpeckers would have been common at the

time 'The Twelve Days of Christmas' first appeared: they were very familiar to Gilbert White, who described the green wood-pecker's call as 'a loud and hearty laugh'. But both species would then have been virtually confined to England and Wales, where-as today great spotted woodpeckers breed close to the northern tip of the Scottish mainland, while green woodpeckers are also found north of the border.

There is, however, some controversy over the status of the green woodpecker in Scotland during the nineteenth century. Several writers, including Yarrell, asserted that the species was 'common and well-known in the wooded districts of England and Scotland', but other authorities disagreed. It has even been suggested that the existence of a Gaelic name for the green woodpecker – *Lasair choille* – proves it was found north of the border, but, given that this name was also used for the goldfinch, this appears to be a case of mistaken identity, or perhaps wishful thinking.

We do know, though, that the green woodpecker bred near Penrith in the Lake District during the 1880s, and that finally, in 1951, breeding was proven in Scotland, in Selkirk. Today the spe-cies can be found throughout much of the lowlands of south and central Scotland, with a handful of pairs in the true highlands.

The author and naturalist John Lister-Kaye, based at the Aigas Field Centre near Beauly, just north of the Great Glen, tells me that:

> we tend to treat it as a rare vagrant, but, like the nuthatch, there
> is now evidence that greens are nudging their way north. I'm told

that green woodpeckers are now regular around Edinburgh, and I suspect that climate change will bring them north more and more.

Ironically the spread of the green woodpecker may be linked with the success of an alien (albeit long-established) British mammal, the rabbit. Rabbits crop the grass short, which suits woodpeckers as it enables them to find and gain access to ants' nests, which are in any case commoner where the turf is shorter. The rapid rise in rabbit numbers since the 1960s and 1970s, following the eventual control of myxomatosis, is likely to have helped the birds' northward spread.

Great spotted woodpeckers likewise extended their range northwards during the twentieth century. Ironically, this was following a major decline, especially in north-west England, during the early nineteenth century, probably caused by the highly intensive management of woodlands at the time. But from the 1880s onwards they recolonised southern Scotland and then continued inexorably north, finally reaching Caithness – a county with very few trees – in the 1940s.

They were perhaps given a boost by one of the greatest environmental disasters to hit the British countryside, the spread of Dutch Elm Disease in the 1960s and 1970s, which provided a glut of dead trees where the birds could make their nest-holes. Yet even though the dead elms have long since been felled, great spotted numbers have since continued to rise, with the latest figures suggesting there are at least 140,000 breeding pairs in Britain – almost three times the total for green woodpeckers.

The story of the third British breeding woodpecker, the diminutive, sparrow-sized lesser spotted, could hardly be a greater contrast. Once known as the 'barred woodpecker', to reflect the difference in pattern from its larger cousin the 'pied' or great spotted, this shy, elusive species has seen its numbers plummet in recent years, after also gaining a brief boost from Dutch Elm Disease. With just 1,500 breeding pairs remaining, there is a real possibility that, during the next few decades, the lesser spotted woodpecker will join the wryneck and disappear as a British breeding bird.

Whereas its larger relatives have adapted well to living in wooded parks and gardens, the lesser spotted remains essentially a woodland species, though it is sometimes seen in the larger London green spaces such as Richmond and Bushy Parks. Yet the pioneering eighteenth-century French naturalist Georges-Louis Leclerc, Comte de Buffon, observed that 'in winter this species draws near houses and vine-yards, that it shelters in holes of trees, and sometimes disputes possession with the Coal Titmouse, which it compels to give up its lodging.' I have occasionally seen them in winter, tagging on to the end of a mixed flock of tits and goldcrests, increasing their chances of finding food.

Right up to the middle of the last century, lesser spotted woodpeckers were also often found in orchards, which have mainly been grubbed out in recent decades. So perhaps their retreat to woodlands is more a sign of their increased rarity than any wider preference for habitat – scarce birds are often found only in their optimum habitat, whereas when a species' fortunes are on the rise, overcrowding makes them less fussy.

The loss of the lesser spotted from wide swathes of the English countryside – there are now only a handful of breeding pairs in my home county of Somerset – is down to the usual factors: poor management of woodlands, a decline of orchards, and habitat loss. Most of all, it seems, it is down to a shortage of food. This is especially problematic during the breeding season, when chicks have been known to starve in the nest. When this happens, over time the population of this sedentary species in any given area inexorably falls.

Others have suggested that the rise of the larger and more dominant great spotted woodpecker may be to blame, but I suspect that the contrasting change in their fortunes is simply coincidental, rather than a genuine cause of the smaller species' decline. William Yarrell's statement that the lesser spotted woodpecker 'is not uncommon around London, and may be seen in Kensington Gardens' – indeed, a hundred years or so ago this was the commonest of the three woodpeckers in London – seems incredible today.

All three British woodpeckers have, as you might expect for such attractive birds, a wealth of folk-names. The green woodpecker is the champion in that department, with more than fifty recorded names, which mostly fall into three categories: their habits and habitat, their distinctive call, and their reputation as weather forecasters.

In the first group are self-explanatory names such as 'hewhole' and 'pick-a-tree'. The second includes several variations on the same theme – 'laughing bird', 'yaffingale' and 'yaffle' – the last still occasionally heard in rural areas. When he was a toddler, my son Charlie would call the green woodpeckers in our garden 'the birds that laugh at me', and it is true that the call does sound rather like (occasionally hysterical) laughter – it reminds me of the character Muttley in the 1960s cartoon series *Wacky Races*.

Another group of folk-names for the species derives from the widespread belief that woodpeckers in general, and the green in particular, call when it is about to rain. They include 'rain bird', 'rain fowl' and 'weather cock', and in Somerset, the more prosaic 'wet-wet' or simply 'wet bird'.

This may link back to an ancient belief, reported by the Victorian ornithologist William Swainson. This says that when God finished creating the Earth, he ordered the birds to dig holes to create seas, lakes and ponds. All but the woodpecker obeyed, so he was condemned to spend the rest of eternity digging holes in trees, and drinking nothing but rain water. Hence, Swainson believed, the legend of the rain bird: the woodpecker is forever calling to the clouds to ask for rain, to receive in its open beak the drops that fall from the sky.

It may well be the case that woodpeckers do call more when rain is due; yet in my book *Birds and Weather* I suggested that the connection may perhaps have arisen because of better acoustics before rain arrives (the calm before the storm), which allowed us to hear the sound more clearly. Another reason why woodpeckers of several species are linked with storms and wet weather right across Europe may be because their drumming sounds like thunder. Whatever the reason, the Romans believed it too: they called woodpeckers *Pluviae avies*, because they are supposed to call more loudly and persistently before rain.

A final category of folk-names for the green woodpecker includes 'woodspite' or 'wood-speight', and 'woodwele' (with many different spellings). While it is tempting to assume this relates to the bird's habitat, Yarrell maintained that it is more likely to be a corruption of 'woad', referring to the bird's green plumage, and *Specht*, the German word for 'woodpecker'. In an odd twist, 'woodwele' and its variants are thought to refer to the call of another species, the golden oriole, whose females are surprisingly similar in colour and appearance to the green woodpecker.

In contrast, the great spotted and lesser spotted woodpeckers only have a handful of folk-names, including 'French pie', 'wood pie', 'little wood pie' (for lesser spotted, of course) and the similar 'witwall' and 'hickwall' respectively.

There is one other woodpecker species that haunts the British birding scene. The black woodpecker is Europe's largest species, weighing almost twice as much as its nearest rival the green woodpecker, and reaching a length of up to 22 inches (55 cm).

With its all-black plumage, apart from an ivory-coloured bill, pale, staring eye and bright crimson cap, you might think that any reports of the species on this side of the Channel would be quickly accepted by the relevant authorities. Yet even though there were at least eighty sightings before 1959 (mostly during the Victorian era), and a handful of reports since, the black woodpecker has still never been confirmed as occurring in a wild state in Britain. That is despite the fact that in recent years the species has expanded its range in Europe, and can now be found in suitable habitat in northern France, Belgium and the Netherlands, right up to the Channel coast.

Much as I would love this magnificent woodpecker to be added to the 'British List' of birds recorded here in the wild, I suspect it may never be. Past records are probably either errors of identification, escaped or deliberately released birds, or fraudulent records – Victorian collectors would have paid a high premium for a specimen supposedly shot in Britain. But maybe one day a birder sitting on a Kentish headland will stare out to sea in disbelief, as a black woodpecker lands exhausted on the shingle beach below, having just flown across the Channel.

This huge, crow-like bird first came to the attention of the British public in 1955, via the new medium of television. The black woodpecker was one of the stars of a short black-and-white film, 'Carpenters of the Forest'. Made by a German naturalist, Heinz Sielmann, this was featured on the weekly wildlife BBC TV series *Look*, presented by Peter Scott. Scott had been struck by the pioneering techniques used by Sielmann, which included remarkably intimate views from *inside* the birds' nest-holes – something that had never even been attempted, let alone shown, before.

With just one channel available to the viewing public, *Look* was watched by millions. But even so, no-one was prepared for the response to Sielmann's film: callers jammed the BBC switchboard asking to see it again, and the programme's AI (Appreciation Index) was one of the highest of the year. As a result, Sielmann was given the apt nickname 'Mr Woodpecker'.

Epilogue

During almost two-and-a-half centuries since 'The Twelve Days of Christmas' was first published, in words that are recognisably like the version we still sing today, Britain and its birds have undergone extraordinary changes.

In 1780, our countryside was mostly farmed using a system of open fields, radiating out from each town or village, without boundaries such as hedgerows. Then, within a few decades, the Enclosure Acts transformed rural Britain forever. By switching from the old method of strip-farming, with the land held in common by the local people, to a patchwork quilt of hedge-bound fields, each owned by individual landowners, enclosure transformed both the rural landscape and the lives of working people. This, in turn, created new opportunities for some species of birds, and reduced them for others.

Soon afterwards, following the onset of the Industrial Revolution, Britain switched in a remarkably short time from a mainly rural, agrarian society to a largely urban one. This happened at an astonishing speed: within just two or three generations a nation of country-dwellers became citizens of a new, metropolitan society.

One unpredictable consequence of this change was that the British developed a deep love of, and connection with, the natural world. Perhaps this came about through nostalgia amongst city-dwellers for the rural life their parents and grandparents had left behind; or maybe it was because of the increase in both their wealth and leisure time, brought about by more prosperous jobs in towns and cities.

Whatever the reasons, the following century saw a huge rise in interest in nature. And because birds are so visible, and so ubiquitous, birdwatching – or birding as it is now known – became one of the most widely enjoyed recreational activities of the modern era.

One of the great paradoxes of this, as I hope *The Twelve Birds of Christmas* has demonstrated, is that at the same time as a passion for birds and birding has increased, many of the species that live in our countryside have decreased in numbers. It's not all bad news: some species featured in the Christmas carol, such as the blackbird, are thriving, often thanks to the food and shelter we provide in our gardens. But others, notably the grey partridge and turtle dove, are heading towards the brink of extinction as British birds.

Yet I remain an optimist. The very fact that we have such a deep affection for birds, both as living creatures and as cultural emblems, suggests to me that we will ultimately manage to reverse the declines of these special creatures.

I hope you have enjoyed reading about the twelve birds I have featured in this book as much as I enjoyed researching and writing about them. They are all, in their own way, unique; they all combine fascinating biological behaviour with deep cultural resonance; and they all matter to many millions of people.

Whether you agree or not with my avian interpretation of this popular carol, this quest has presented me with the chance to inform, educate and, I hope, entertain you with the stories of twelve remarkable and fascinating birds, all of which deserve our attention and care.

So, next time you stand in a church, school or on a doorstep, and begin to sing that famous opening line, 'On the first day of Christmas, my true love gave to me . . .', spare a thought for the grey partridge, turtle dove, chicken, blackbird, yellowhammer, goose, swan, nightjar, crane, black grouse, sandpiper and woodpecker – the twelve very special birds of Christmas . . .

Acknowledgements

As always, I'd like to thank the team at Square Peg (an imprint of Penguin Random House): Rowan Yapp, who commissioned the book and steered it through publication; Dinah Drazin, Lily Richards and Rosie Palmer from the design team, as well as Konrad Kirkham, Fiona Brown and Harriet Dobson. The lovely cover image is by Neil Gower.

Professor Jeremy Dibble of the University of Durham gave me very helpful advice on the origins of the carol.

Graham Coster once again edited the book, offering useful suggestions and advice as always, while my agent Broo Doherty was her usual rock of strength. Thanks especially to her colleague David Headley at DHH Literary Agency, who suggested the idea for the book.

Finally, I'd like to thank my wife Suzanne and children David, James, Charlie, George and Daisy for their love and support.

List of Illustrations

The majority of these images came from books sourced from The London Library. Our thanks go to them for their wonderful collection.

pp.ii, 5, 117, 182, from *An Illustrated Manual of British Birds* by Howard Saunders (London: Gurney and Jackson, 1889)

pp.iii, v, 214 © Natalia Slavetskaya

pp.8, 26, 44, 62, 76, 92, 110, 146, 162, 176, 192, from *1800 Woodcuts by Thomas Bewick and His School* edited by Blanche Cirker (New York: Dover Publications, Inc., 1962)

pp.14, 32, 87, 141, 167, 197, from *British Birds in their Haunts* by Rev. C. A. Johns (London: Society for Promoting Christian Knowledge, 1918)

p.22, from *Familiar Wild Birds* by W. Swaysland (London: Cassell and Company Ltd, 1903)

pp.29, 55, 69, 108, 114, 152, from *Old English Cuts and Illustrations for Artists and Craftspeople* by Bowles & Carver (New York: Dover Publications, Inc., 1970)

pp.47, 50 © Shutterstock

pp. 41, 75, 99, 128, from *The Birds of Essex* by Miller Christy (Chelmsford: Edmund Durrant & Co., 1890)

pp.80, 204, from *A History of British Birds* by Howard Saunders (London: John Van Voorst)

pp.125, 134, from *Beautiful Birds Described* by Rev. Robert Tyas (London: Madwick, Houlston & Co., Ltd, 1854-6)

p.156, from *Treasury of Animal Illustrations from Eighteenth-Century Sources* by Carol Belanger Grafton (New York: Dover Publications, Inc., 1988)

p.173, from *Bird-Life of the Borders* by Abel Chapman (London: Gurney and Jackson, 1889)

pp.180, 188, from *The Handbook of British Birds* by H. F. Witherby (London: H. F. & G. Witherby Ltd, 1940)

p.211, from *A Dictionary of Birds* by Alfred Newton (London: Adam and Charles Black, 1893-6)